IN THE COMPANY
OF
RUSSELL ATKINS

A celebration by friends
on his 90th birthday

Edited by Diane Kendig and

Robert E. McDonough

Inspired and assisted by Russell Atkins,
the best editor

Introduction by George Bilgere

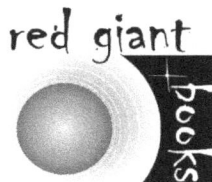

red giant
books

CONTENTS

TWO PREFACES BY THE EDITORS

Preface One

A long with Bob McDonough, I was asked to edit this tribute anthology for Russell Atkins' 90th birthday, with the goal of gathering an array of poets who have felt the influence of Atkins' life and work and who wanted to share their gratitude for that influence.

The first poets to my mind were those from the mid-1970s to 80s in Cleveland workshops and readings when I first knew Russell. However, I was aware that Russell had a poetry life long before me, in the 1950s through the early '70s as editor of *Free Lance* and teacher of young poets for the Ohio Arts Council, Karamu House, and, along with Norman Jordan, the Muntu poets. Three teenagers from then who still write today as grown men contributed to this anthology: Hzal Anubewei, Yaseen As-Sami, and M.A. Shaheed. Norman Jordan's work is here posthumously, thanks to his family. From this period, Russell asked us to contact Lewis Turco, Robert Fleming, and Nathan Oliver, who appear here, along with three others I'd like to mention.

While researching this early period of Russell's career in the Russell Atkins Archives at the Atlanta University Center, I found a bittersweet announcement of another tribute anthology, one for the legal defense of Jim Lowell, the book dealer prosecuted for selling "obscene literature," which is to say, the poetry of the time. First on the list of contributors, alphabetically, is Russell Atkins, followed by 30 others, including Kent Taylor and of course, d.a. levy, himself being prosecuted and persecuted for poetry then. Also in the Atkins Archives, I found a letter from Russell as editor of *Free Lance*, accepting a poem by one Chris Franke, and a news clipping about a protest reading with P. K. Saha. Those long-standing Atkins friends Taylor, Franke, and Saha join us in this anthology.

Russell was clearly beloved and respected by the 1970s-1980s generation of poets when I first knew him, and among the poets in this anthology from that period are John Stickney, John Donoghue, Zena Zipporah, Mary Weems, Ray McNiece, John Gabel, Joan Nicholl, Mwatabu Okantah, Leatrice Emeruwa, and the editor of Russell's fine book, *Here in The*, Leonard Trawick.

Meanwhile, I found a whole new generation of poets who were devotees of Russell's work. First among them are Kevin Prufer and Michael Dumanis whose recent book, *Russell Atkins: On the Life and Work of an American Master* (Pleiades), has renewed interest in Atkins. As I googled the current Russell Atkins turf, I found references to him in a course at U.C.-Berkeley, and in a *New York Times* shout-out for the Prufer-Dumanis Pleiades books, as well as other signs that newcomers are reading Atkins. We contacted as many of them as we could and those who responded are here. Along with a new tribute by Kevin and Michael, we have Caryl Pagel, Ra Washington, and Dawn Lundy Martin.

As the work was accumulating, Russell received a typewriter. Slowly he pecked out his first line, "Will I write?" Days later, he began a poem, originally titled "Rest Home." For weeks when we visited, he would be working on it, in hand writing. I would type it up and bring back copy, but Russell would be several versions past that version. At one point, Bob heard Russell say with a chuckle, "Let's complicate this a little." He finally declared it finished, and it appears here for the first time in print as "Dawn," along with a few Atkins poems from the 1980s *Chestnutt Record* that have not yet appeared in book form or online. And so our anthology has several new and previously uncollected Atkins poems.

We wanted someone with the gravitas, goodwill, and objectivity to say a few words about Russell's poetry, and we invited George Bilgere, who has graciously provided us with his wonderful introduction to the poetry of Russell Atkins for those who may not be familiar with it and for all who can appreciate Bilgere's fine ear and articulate appreciation.

Taken together, the result is this book. It is not a comprehensive anthology containing work by all of Russell's friends, just 28 of us. It does not represent a unified school of poetry by a long shot, not in style nor content. You might think that Atkins' fans would write like him, but if we learned anything at all from Russell, it is the poet must write like himself or herself and not like anyone else nor the latest poetry movement. Let the critics be damned—and damn him some did—and let time tell. We believe that time has served Atkins' work well because he first served the work. So may we all. And may our many differences herein reflect his good model.

In addition to our differences, some commonalities hold the collection together, too. First, there are several Cleveland poems. These are not imitative of Russell's Cleveland poems, but an indication that many of us, like him, have spent time in that city. Also, several poems about Russell or addressed to Russell surface throughout the book. Then there are the tributes each poet contributed, which are the true glue binding our book, the way the presence of Russell Atkins and his poetry have bound us at times in real time and for now, in this anthology. We present this work to him and to our readers, with thanks.

Diane Kendig

3

Preface Two

Diane Kendig and I have both known Russell Atkins for about forty years. That puts us slightly on the long side of the middle in terms of length of friendship. Some of our contributors have not met Russell, only admired his work. A number have known him a decade or so longer than Diane and I. And one remembers Russell from high school. But all admire Russell's work and his long and generous dedication to it, and all, I believe, feel grateful to be able to contribute to honoring him. And the editors feel grateful for having been able to bring all these poets together.

In case you're wondering, there is no "School of Atkins" in this anthology, or out of it, either. The poems here are offerings in honor of Russell Atkins, not imitations of his work. You will see very quickly that they come from a diverse group of poets; the editors feel that a book of good poetry will be a more than sufficient tribute to Russell Atkins' life and work.

Diane's "Preface" may give a slight idea of how much good, hard work she has put into this anthology. I have trailed along behind her, doing my best to keep her in sight, learning a lot. It has been a pleasure and a privilege to work with her.

Robert E. McDonough

Part I

Russell Atkins

"Russell was the voice of our GPS."

-John Stickney

Introduction

"How Such Cheerfuls Me":
The Poetry of Russell Atkins

I'll start with a Russell Atkins poem that reflects the qualities I admire most in his work: humor, pathos, and tenderness. An inimitable musicality and a deep, emphatic understanding of the human condition. Here's his portrait of a former beauty queen facing middle age:

Now Sweet Cathy

Now sweet Cathy
Is pouring beer here in a bar
Pouring beer in a bar
Where hard workers are.
Endure costs her; her dreams fewer,
Cathy with promoted bust is mature.

Cathy, ceased now
In yielding of honey,
Is dedicated to her
Baby and steady money.

Cathy, I shall cruel.
You will old, you will woe.
And beer obnoxious grows,
Hard workers drear.
Cathy, Cathy! (she's too mature to hear)
Could I but whisper in her ear:

Reality's IS, is but Is alone.
We confect it a body
For the bones!

Just about every enthusiastic reader of poetry has at one time or another encountered Keats's famous sonnet, "On First Looking Into Chapman's Homer," with its magnetic lines describing how the young poet felt when encountering the great translation: "Then felt I like some watcher of the skies / When a new planet swims into his ken." Which is pretty much exactly how I felt when I encountered, much too late, the poetry of Russell Atkins. And mentioning Atkins, an African American poet from Cleveland, and the 19th century British Romantic in the same breath is not at all odd. The young Keats was an omnivorous reader who ploughed through the classics and his contemporaries with a ferocious need to absorb and master their rhythms and cadences. I hear in the work of Russell Atkins precisely the same hunger, the same burning desire to listen to the poetry of the past and of his own time, to find in it what works for his own purposes.

The great Jesuit poet Gerard Manley Hopkins once defined poetry as language that aspires to the condition of music, and in Atkins we hear this again and again. He's not always interested in making sense, in writing a literally coherent narrative. I'd suggest rather that his intention is to create sound structures, assemblages of words in which motifs of music and rhythm stand in for conventional notions of sense and meaning. And he accomplishes this, to an astonishing degree, by listening to echoes, fragments, bits and pieces of modern masters and assembling them in highly musical language collages. To read Atkins is to take a kind of audio tour of the history of modern poetry.

For instance, listen to these starkly imagistic lines from William Carlos Williams' poem, "The Great Figure," in which he describes a fire truck as it rushes toward a fire:

> I saw the figure 5
> in gold
> on a red
> firetruck
> moving
> tense
> unheeded
> to gong clangs
> siren howls
> and wheels rumbling...

Now here's Atkins, from "Air Disaster":

there in a thunder
a too thick of aghasts of dust
over the field—
ambulances, fire's fire!!!
roundabout dancing
and a siren flamingly
eeeeeeeee s

It's the images here--specifically, as Williams would say, the "objects," rather than any idea--that carry the poem, along with the distinctively stark and topiary syntax. But in Atkins' hands the imagery seems, at least to my ear, much more musical and emotionally engaging. The language dances.

There's also an echo of the distinctive music of E.E. Cummings. "Aghasts of dust," in which the adjective "aghast" is alchemized into a noun, is a characteristic Atkins trope by way of Cummings. Atkins is probably thinking of "my father moved through dooms of love / through sames of am through haves of give." And Cummings' famously disruptive, outlaw punctuation shows up lines like this, from Atkins' "Abstractive," in which memories are "compilingly / length',d into the poor pale."

And here's a stanza from Atkins' "Elegy to a Hurt Bird That Died" which, to my ear at least, soars with the stratospheric grandiloquence of his fellow Clevelander, Hart Crane:

I suppose you suppose, as some,
It was one of the lone
Who did this. Ah yes,
As if one's boned
Skeletal'd in uneager sands
On shores undroned.

Do I hear the organ notes of Crane's "At Melville's Tomb," where the surge of language breaks and shatters into brittle shards against the rocky limits of meaning?

Often beneath the wave, wide from the ledge
The dice of drowned men's bones he saw bequeath

An embassy. Their numbers as he watched,
Beat on the dusty shore and were obscured.

And clearly Atkins knows his Ezra Pound, and the Master's
Imagist anthology chestnut, "In a Station of the Metro":

"The apparition of those face in the crowd;
Petals on a wet, black bough."

Here's Atkins, modulating and expanding with his own vari-
ations, in "Evening Reflections In A Birdbath":

"still   there in our birdbath
strangely eye-like   light
repeated from the sky…"

There's another kind of music, a darker one, in his poem,
Idyll":

snow brings restraint
and takes you by the arm:
snow's religious, morals over
the landscape, relaxes
with a minister's smile
and its hands folded
across a great belly…

The austere and portentous tone of these lines is an homage
to Emily Dickinson, and her famous evocation of winter:

There's a certain slant of light,
Winter Afternoons—
That oppresses, like the Heft
Of Cathedral Tunes…

When it comes, the Landscape listens--
Shadows—hold their breath…

And one last example brings us back to the music master
himself, the language maestro, tinkerer, and Jesuit jazz man,
Hopkins. Here's the beginning of Atkins' "It's Here In The," as
he reacts to a news story about a train disaster:

Here in the newspaper—wreck of the East Bound.

A photograph bound to bring on cardiac asthenia.
There is a blur that mists the pages:
On one side's a gloom of dreadful harsh,
Then breaks flash lights up sheer.
There is much huge about. I suppose
   those no 's are people
  between that suffering of—
  (what have we more? for Christ's sake!...

The language here, with its compressed and fractured syntax, reflects the "sprung rhythm" of Hopkins' own famous response to a newspaper story, this one about a tragic shipwreck, "The Wreck of the Deutschland," which sounds like this:

But how shall I...make me a room there:
Reach me a...Fancy, come faster--
Strike you the sight of it? look at it loom there,
Thing that she...there then! The Master,
Ipse, the only one, Christ, King...

This is what makes Russell Atkins such a richly satisfying and exciting poet to read. On the one hand, he's a highly literary poet, a craftsman of the highest order who, like the High Modernists—Eliot, Pound, Yeats—appropriates elements of past traditions to, in Pound's words, "make it new." But he's also very much a creature of his time, a jazz man and musician. His poetry demands to be read aloud. Its music, full of twitchy rhythms and beguiling turns, transcends the merely programmatic, the earth-bound demands of the agitator, the reformer, the crusader. Atkins' wide-ranging verbal experiments, his erudition, allow his poems to rise above the strict limitations of mere subject, mere politics and propaganda, to become as infinitely meaningful as music itself. Unlike many of his contemporaries, like Langston Hughes or d.a. levy, he's not a "Cleveland poet." He's not a "political poet." No modifiers required. Russell Atkins is a poet. His work has gone unread for far too long, and it's wonderful to hear his full-throated, resonant language rising again. Like the sparrow in your back yard, announcing spring after a long winter.

I'll close with a stanza from an Atkins poem called "World'd Too Much (Irritable Song). The title, of course, echoes Word-

sworth's poem cautioning us against the dangers of being se-
duced away from the natural world by sheer materialism; but
here we see Atkins, a poet of the city, finding solace, not in na-
ture, but in the mysterious pleasures of being the only passenger
on the bus at the end of the day:

> Bus hollows on of back windows
> awidth'd where oxygen, gust'd,
> crosswise of neglect, a joyous'd
> foregone of seats, the while a beer can's
> joust'd about the floor's rubbish'd
> and a driver's on the last run
> as of fatal'd alone—
>
> how such cheerfuls me!

George Bilgere

Russell Atkins

New Poems

We are fortunate to have these poems by Russell Atkins: "DAWN REST HOME" was written in 2015. "HOMELESS." "OVER HIS DEAD BODY," and "THRENODIC FANTASIES FOR EXAMPLE" appeared in Nathan Oliver's *Chestnutt Review*. This is their first appearance in a book.

DAWN Rest Home

hag'd like of laughter. . .
laughter that hags

now and then
down the hall
more laughing hag'd

--thither of lit
is of a room thus'd to odd
with about's of shadow'd
a door's nearby of at
of in, or out, or of a door's <u>from</u>

COLD OPEN
        on <u>somewhere</u>

        aloud voices Next
GOOD morning, good morning
GOOD morning, sir,
GOOD morning all,
          (Good (Oh Really
             Who says so?)

beheld as day "dares" up to up'd
      then falls
            to eve'd

meanwhile
then and now
hag'd laugh

Homeless

His less barber'd hair vagabonds
as of more slept
too much in parks:
old friends would flee
him if they glimpsed
how far his veer
from sprawled houses
that flaunt their lavish,
from golf courts, Mercedes,
cocktail parties

he's somebody yore,
flunk'd of fortune
--but a bag now
folded to shred!

he may despond
to a lake's like a sea
that's luminous but not of cheer
and gives a bath
--then sleep

Over His Dead Body

of him,
milk in a years of sieved gush:
a threnody'd squawk of chickens,
of hundreds squabbled to grocers from farms;
stiffened in hellos of stoves, at last,
as trundled bones on plates that lair
         -- all this:
crack'd apart of eggs, babes against
affrightful skillets glee'd by grease:
nameless butchers that pummell'd
the gory steaks for abrupt of his fork
and teeth; unravelled bacon by the yard
moving its char along his tubes,
could not be held, could not leave much;
oysters could not save a thing;
nor could shrimp from plundered shallows,
neckbones, heavy pork chops,
do much – nor could groundround
daunt; steamed up lobster,
lush'd with butter, failed completely
 -- the body no gravy could fill
to be morsel'd off to fat grubs
(Let my own personal feelings offend:
that he ate well enough we know
-- as to what end -- ,

Threnodic Phantasies for Example:

For somebody woeful's close to Cypress'd,
vaunt at its dirged through a fabric:
      sumptuously, be about to dine. Say:
Chateau d'Yquem, 1928 (zap a coroner
with gastric'd wow); "Chartreuse of pheasant,
charlotte glaze with strawberries,
--ile flottante and poires Alma";
Bifteck bourguignon—add, squab!
          of course,
expire as of beheld of fabulous'd:
Renoir'd glens, Rembrandts, Theotokopoulos,
Delacroix—that's for anybody
of willow'd to lorn Cypress'd!
or tell of a sudden for travels:
aloft villa'd above a lake's sheen'd lapse
in Portugal, Switzerland's steeps
ski'd upon as thousand'd Alp'd;
of browsed gardens, the Castello Balduino
         at Montalto di Pavia
--the Caribbean next
slendering in palms!

truth? From someone woeful'd close to Cypress?

one too close to Cypress'd
should talk of a fabled of friends:
when they ask, "How's what's-name doin"?
you only know his most: tell them
there's precious less than a Rolls-Royce;
a phone that Wall Street's its ring;

Madison Aved, or Manhattan'd offices
Head of a Bank with abounds of secretariesd
obsequious'd hither with hie,'d,
                    or of late, say
retired to Bermuda proned of by sea!
(the Queen yet visits – ah!)
fugues of music, John Bach's,
by all means, shall full at The End
in a bier'd church

Part II

In His Company

"Oh, what good company poets are!"

--José Martí

Hzal Anubewei

Russell's Influence

I met Russell Atkins attending a poetry reading given by Muntu Writers at John Hay High School in spring of 1968 along with Norman Jordan. It was the first time I had ever heard Black Poetry. I was hooked. The one thing I remember Russell said to me was "Anthony, why do you want to be a poet, they don't make any money." Russell's approach to poetry was the most revolutionary form of writing I have ever encountered even until this day. He has inspired me since I met him. A truly wonderful human being.

Eyes

The
eyes of creation
are closed
in deep memory
Love's breeze stirs the urge to exist
without pause
Mysterious shadows pour through
the veils of Maya
Space is the soil of creation
Elements of carbon
rise
pouring shade into boiling pits
of hydrogen, nitrogen, and oxygen
Galaxy size mountains of red yellow gas collide
splashing color on trillions of suns
Listen to the music
Listen to the music
spinning in space
The
eyes
of creation are open
in
deep memory
urged to exist
the breeze of love released
without pause
without hesitation
forever

Father

in memory of my father William J Fudge Sr.

I
am the father
who was the son
My
day is upon me.
In my hands are the obligations
the working tools of manhood passed on to me.
Just before sunrise I meditate
HaHiYa speak wisdom to me.
When my wife looks at me let love shine
When my children call
let a smile be on their face

I
am the father
who was the son.
Now
I am a citizen
son of my people
son of a nation
I carry iron the work men must do
I pray for the fathers that fight to keep us free
The word love beats on my chest
Across my shoulders is a harness
like my father I must learn to pull my weight
Carry the water of life
until my days are done
Embracing both sorrow and joy
arms on the same body
at night just after moonrise
I gather my family
hold them for just a little while
tell them what I know of wisdom

I
am the father
who once was the child
I
am the father
who was the son

Pouring Shade

Pour
some shade on the road
to cool my feet
pour some on my hands
tired from the week
pour some sweet shade on my head
I need some relief
Let it flow like honey
       drip like maple syrup
serve me a glass of lemonade
stirred to the taste of sweet shade
Pour it over everything
Pour it on a rainbow
Even
the colors of nature want to know
how it feels to taste sweet

Yaseen AsSami

Russell, my mentor

I have known Russell since the Mid-1960's when I was part of the Muntu workshop, an inner city project conducted by Norman Jordan and Russell Atkins in the old O.I.C. Building on Superior Avenue. Its participants included young people like Bill Russell, John Hall, Clyde Shy, Marty Freeman, and many others I have not mentioned. I was guided by Russell and the others to develop my own style and my gift to express myself through writing. He was then and is now a very good friend and mentor. He gave me confidence and courage to move forward with my writing and to stay the course. He has a good vision of the creative nature of people. Russell is a fantastic poet, one of my favorites.

Putting a Twenty On a Ten

Guns blazing lights flashing children screaming
Junebug crying
What you doing Billy???

He say . I be puttin a 20 on a10.
Dumb negros everywhere.
Scraping the last remains of a lullaby forgotten
Off the bottom of a Blues opera
Humming the star spangle banner and whispering lies
About the trials and troubles
Of Jesus The Christ
Spitting into the wind and caressing sorrows
What you doing.?.
Junebug!!Billy!
They say we be puttin twenty on ten
Clang clang
Buzz buz
Zip wiz rumble young man rumble
I stand here in the middle of nowhere
Being restricted by someone trying to get to a place where
All things are unlimited
Bang Bang Bang
                    What the Hell??? Putting A 20 A10.

A Glass of Lemonade

Oh just for a glass of lemonade.
I would snatch the tear drops from your eyes
And rip the love from your heart.
Oh for a glass of lemonade.
I would wade through oceans of blood,
And kill the meaning of desire.
I love you more than sunshine,
But less than moonlight,
And lemonade.
Sometimes I find myself crawling through nightmares
Only to be saved by a glass of lemonade.
Tyme snatches the chill from the refrigerator.
My shadow stands shivering screaming for a glass
Of lemonade,
I set at the table talking to my former tymes .
Watching tomorrow make love to a glass of lemonade.
Wandering through Charlie's mind.
Kicking over trash cans of ideals, burning
Old newspapers .
Terror trembles in the path of death.
Fate hides behind yesterday's excuses,
Watching angry butterflies fling grenades at dead horses.
While drinking a glass of lemonade
Observing paper progenies play chubby in piles of broken
hearts.
Bowls. Bells. Birds sing songs of joy
I sit wondering why love wears a mask of lunacy.
Running through a blues song canoodling camels

RAC--IT!! !

Moving closer to the tyme when Willie-B will come?

    BLAM!

KA-CHING
    WHAM
        BOOM
SCHWICH

                           o RING! RING!

    CLANG!!!

Suddenly the door slams and the window breaks.,
    BOOM! !.
        CRACKLE

        PING

I Hear someone singing in the background.
    who is it?
        WHO IS IT?
            WHO THE HELL? IS IT ?
CLANG
    CLANG
        CLANG
    POO-NANNY ! !
            STOP THAT RAC-IT,

one long one short two tweets and a whistle and a tear
    somewhere between now and then
    close to never lost between commitment and self
destruct
    stands the empty vessel that father called a heart
        further on down the road you will accompany
    me
    in a space and tyme close to a lost luve and a scream
i stand whispering into a place where life has no mearing or purpose

John Donoghue

On Russell

Long before I met Russell I came across a copy of *Here in The*, a book that stopped me cold in my poetry-writing tracks: "What's the point of me writing any poetry," I thought, "when Mr. Russell Atkins is writing poetry like this?" His use of language was entirely original—and wonderful. With my grammar-challenged brain I couldn't explain to myself *what* he was doing, and when I tried to do it myself—I couldn't do that either. I still can't explain it, or do it, but so what? Russell does it, and his doing it puts it in the world. Here are some examples: "where an oncoming diesel/dangerouses;" "the lively soiled dishes/pile the food cart with obstacle," "I came upon that gate/that tracery'd gently into open," "On one side's a gloom of dreadful harsh,/Then brakes flash lights up sheer./There is much huge about," "Afresh'd with paint, the shop had glare," "came:/to sight drastic'd a lo and behold." It was as if he'd found a new dimension to the language of poetry, opened up a new seam in it, and I've often gone back to that book, that seam, not to mine it myself but to marvel at it, and be nurtured by it.

27

In the design review meeting He said

it *isn't* perfect—in fact I'll even admit it's a bit
fucked-up here and there. OK!—maybe more
than just a bit, maybe more than just here and there,
setting off a bang like that
definitely not my best. But look, we're stuck with it,

committed, and hey!, time works, I like time, and physics,
chemistry, the dynamics of it all—
good, huh?—
and photosynthesis—not bad—all the water, rain, the clouds,
the sky in general, day and night, rising moons—all that

I foresaw, that's mine. And color!, the senses, compassion,
sex!—sex is good, right?, they *love* sex! OK—perfect/
not-so-perfect. And yeah, death's a problem—all the killing,
maiming, eating,
all the just plain dying—blindsided, never saw it coming.

And their brains? Well, fatty, gelatinous—
it wasn't me who said gelatinous.
So, OK. What do you want to do?...Crucify me?
Funny.
Stop production? Close our doors? It *works*, they *won't* sue,

they don't *want* to sue—they *blame themselves*.
Yeah, I know, I'm outta here, but I'll be fine—
it will finally blow,
and there's nothing in this model that connects designer
to design.

Solstice

My neighbor's attic light is on again. It happens
maybe twice a year: a bare bulb hanging
from a cord, its stark light
reflected off the rafters' silvered insulation
giving to my upstairs hall an eerie glow—where I pace,
awake again at three in pain.

Looked at from below, the window
shows only insulation, rafters, and the bulb—
a rough, mechanical intelligence to which I give tonight
the burden of my vanity and rage, my jealousies,
greed, my need to win—the list
endless, my heart dismayed, eager
to be a different heart.

At the roof's peak, the moon is stuck to the sky
like a small bright button, its reflected light,
spread so thin over this world,
is wan, pathetic, diminished by the window.

It takes the twisted shadows of the bare trees, sharp
and shot across the lawns, to finally brighten everything,
the moon's light seeming now pervasive,
deep. My heart will never change,
and I cannot have a different heart. And never
do I tell my neighbors their light is on—it's on for days,
then one night it's off.

Revision

In Rwanda she gave her victims a choice: *Buy the bullet*
I will soon put through your head, or be hacked to death.
And here in this river, she doesn't raise that blue heron
from the shallows, she is the rising heron,
as she is the mother of napalm, destroyer
of the ozone, as she is my eyes that see this glass light
lapping at my feet: I've come to search the bottom
for things magical, and I have a pailful,

but I am sick to death of praising her, and sick
of her illusions—language, consciousness.
Look at me, she says, *and see yourself as separate*
and responsible: I'll *make your body,* you
drop the bomb—then act as if you came from someplace else.
See that desert's beauty?—I dried a sea for it.

Michael Dumanis

On Meeting Russell Atkins

In the autumn of 2007, I became the Director of the Cleveland State University Poetry Center, the press that published Russell Atkins's chapbook *Here in The* in 1976. As I was going over the Center's huge inventory of old poetry titles Russell's slim volume jumped out at me. The cleverly stylized and unexpected turns of language, playful musicality, and spare diction of the collection were really striking. We only had a few copies of the book left—I brought a few on a whim to that year's AWP Book fair in New York and was pleasantly surprised to see all of them enthusiastically snapped up by conference-goers. At the time, Russell was still living alone in a small house on Grand Avenue. I visited him there and was immediately charmed and moved by his intelligence and self-deprecating wit. He took me through multiple shoeboxes of artifacts—issues of journals he had edited forty years prior, correspondence with Marianne Moore and Langston Hughes. I wanted to do something that might help preserve him, his poetry, and his cultural legacy.

The Forecast

I carry myself out into the rainswept blur.
I lift my pleasant voice over the coming flood.
I have nothing to do that I'm going to do.
I keep meaning to purchase a dog. I keep waiting

to email you back. When I see you again will
I know who you are? Once I wove you a mask
of rattan and hair. Once I carved you a mask
of painted wood. I brushed my wooden leg

against your wooden leg. We had learned to imitate
each other's breath. When I see you again will
you know who I am? Will you place your words back
into my open mouth? Once I held you for years

in the stones of my eyes. You were an ineluctable act of
     God.
Into the drainage ditch we hurled our toys.

Squalor

In the beginning, I thought a great deal
about death and sunlight, et cetera,
cramming each syllable that I could cram
into the seconds and brackets allotted me,
all for the memoir that wouldn't be written,
all for the movie that wouldn't be made.
Look at the way I ran after you, arms
stirring dust as you wondered out loud,
glancing up at the skylights, if they needed cleaning.
The walls shed their plaster. Our credit is bad,
and the collection agency has sent its men.
We've had a hard time. We're becoming
a little bit scared. The sudden daughter
shivers through the room. We used to be shiny
and flexible robots. That wasn't a wound
in my back, or a knife, but a key.
The sudden daughter tells us the bad dream:
I tried to kiss him but he had no mouth.
What will be left of her in eighty years.
In the television version of the trials of my life,
the one on all night in a room in my skull,
canned laughter punctuates each time I speak,
the background music swells when I enter.
Does it relieve me or scare me
that I might have made an impression.
If I had a choice, would I rather
tend to a yard or an ocean.
Sometimes one stands in the Mattress King
parking lot, waiting for Rapture.
In Cleveland, I can only get a pierogi
as a topping on my hot dog
when the pierogi chef comes in
but I can always order a pierogi stuffed
inside a sauerkraut and grilled cheese sandwich.
We take a vacation. We get vulnerably drunk.
From time to time, the usual moment
seems endless.

The World

out of blue distances out of closed rooms

out of the pavement and out of the mist

out of the hologram buildings

out of the bright machines and clamor

through the electric landscape we believe in

we wander here we collect ourselves

out of the architecture into the air

likewise in autumn likewise in spring

time pauses long enough for us to tune

the tiny radios inside our chests

we turn them up so we can hear each other

as people come toward us like flashes of light

and tell us the names of the people they love

there are so many flowers

and all of them have names

we move ourselves around them almost dancing

into the stillness and into the wind

breath catching long enough for you to clutch

a stranger's hand

as people drift past us like clouds from a dream

we had once about the sky

Leatrice J.W. Emeruwa

Russell Atkins Tribute

Russell Atkins was the poet "rock-star" at Central High School (Cleveland, Ohio) in the '40's. There were "groupies" clamoring to hear his sonorous and dramatic readings of poetry and gothic short stories every Friday ninth period in the library. I was one. His influence upon my own poetic delivery and continued interest in writing poetry from then on has been paramount. Later in the'70's, he and Jim Kilgore (Tri-C Professor-poet) encouraged me to join them in the nascent Black Arts movement occurring in Cleveland through the group called Ramakha Artists. Of course, Atkins' editorship of *Free Lance*, the outstanding national literary journal for Black writers at the time, provided an incentive for us to produce our very best work for possible publication. Upon reflection, I will say Russell Atkins through his creative output, generous support of beginning artists and generous nature throughout these many years has certainly enthralled hundreds more since his senior high school days.

'bout Mahalia

Is it B.B. or Bobby BluBland
scheduled to sing blues
for Flip's folks on teevee tonight?
No matter.
Mahalia's gonna sing
some down-home gospels to delight
God's folks in heaven!
They ready to get happy
& do a soul dance right now—
all 'em saints gone on before:
Big Maybelle and King Curtis
standing by while
Louie waves his trumpet
in the air & all around
waiting to toot up two storms
as she makes her grand debut.
Dinah, Lady Day, Lucky, Fats,
Ma Rainey, Bessie, and Trane
be ready too.
Ailey, Wes, Jimie, Sam Cooke, Johnny O'Day,
Lil, Coleman, Josh White, Nat "King" Cole
gonna dance, sing or play
in the "welcome" throng.
O, yeah! There's much
joyful noise in heaven
This day cause
Mahalia's on her way—
anxious to sing hallelujah &
Her glad-to-be-home-in-heaven-song.

To My Dark Lover

It will be hard
To let you go
When going-time comes due.
You have plumbed me deep, it's true—
So deep, so deep,
That to think of you
        Is a silent melt
        And a languid spread
        Cell by cell, toe to head
        Of left-over love.
        (Oh, it will be hard to let you go!)

It will be hard
To let you go
When going-time comes due.
You have loved me sweet, it's true—
That to think of you
        Is gold memories
        Of silk kisses soft
        And a wine-thrill glow
        For December's snow.
        (Yes, it will be hard to let you go!)

It will be hard
To let you go
When going-time comes due.
You have marked me much, it's true—
So much, so much
That to think of you
        Is to miss your touch.
        Yet when March winds blow
        And wet-kiss the moon;
        Then going-time is soon!
(And it is so hard to let you go!)

Do the Old Still Love?

Do the old still love?
he asked, smug in his youth
confusing lust with sensibility
"dissing" me.

He really didn't want an answer
was flaunting active testosterone
at his fathers
(be smelling hisself, we elders say).

"Ask yo' mama," I felt like
"dissing" back.
Instead I gave him the evil eye.

Five hundred years—apart
Lord, can we ever bridge
The oceans of our numbness
--respect for wisdom of elders?
respect for ancestors?
respect for selves?

These ain't hip-hop American
Thangs—I know
But look at us.
It don't take no genius to see
We already gon' to hell.

Do the old still love?
Son, sex is good and right,
But it ain't all.
It's praying & caring
heaped-up over the years
by yo' elders
That got us here and keep us yet.

Robert Fleming

In Honor of Russell the Visionary

When I was a very young writer in Cleveland, I met Russell Atkins at a performance at Karamu House, one of the oldest Black theatres in the nation. I was introduced to him by Annetta Jefferson, an accomplished poet-playwright, and immediately fascinated by how he embraced the role of artist. Russell was the dean of the poetry movement at that time, as well as a music theorist, composer, editor, and creator of possibly the oldest black owned poetry magazine, Free Lance.

Conversation with Russell covered a wide range of topics. As a poet, I learned from the master the mechanics of composition, technique, style and content. He refused to be fitted in any category or submit to any ideology. I respected him for that. His theory of "A Psychovisual Perspective for Musical Composition" made more sense to me than Webern, Ives, or Boulez. He is an incredible creative force.

For Russell the Alchemist

Clocks ago – the metropolis demolished
after the exodus of talent and the candle
smothered by two thumbs in the homes of those practicing
art, letters, bohemian frolic, and Bingo:

still groups of poets, playwrights, musicians
shun the sensational for the more introspective
to eager audiences on deserted streets and empty trolleys
ridiculed, unpaid, neglected, and making no difference

Russell the alchemist commands those of us who don't want
to sleep or refuse to belong to commandments of any tribe
while refugees flock from the steel mills to other parts
of the frontier –
yes, these illegals from big box stores like Halle's and Higbee's,

Witness the downtown gathering dust, a large parking lot:
the Great Migration ongoing, we thought we were doing
something bold, something historic

but poets and seers know the past and time are never
forgotten, in time this ghost town will become

what we only imagined.

Cullud Maumau

Cullud maumau

carry platinum daggers to assist old ladies across the street
recite in the mourning from original Madame Fu Fattan dream-
books
speak tunes of buckwheat from fat purple lips
rest with a beer on a baobab tree
embrace the warm of sunlines
dream restlessly of round eye

Cullud maumau

love and hate the siren songs of the bourgeoisie
feast on snake eggs cola nuts and grits
square dance to a different rhythm
know by rote the hollers of Miles and Trane
find religion on panama red
remember the blessings of saltpeter

Cullud maumau

practice magic in blackface
smile NuNile love
drink palm wine toasts to the Prince of Darkness
charleston daily
regret everything you've ever done
dream of the rich with their houses on the hill.

666

Sometimes we forget to wear something over our minds
Accustomed to warm weather
It was considered bad taste to weep over past acts
The end always came first
We had been told to live at our own risk
To keep walking and never look back

Drinking to seduce our tears
We doubted our original sins
And wanted nothing of life but fast songs
Our hearts remained chilled
Eager to dance we sought the hot glow of the fire
Young to ignorance we burned and became memories

Mute the flowers so that the moans can be heard
Stop the march so the dead can get off their feet
Give us the remedy.

Chris Franke

On Russell Atkins

Russell says, "Do not encourage 'economy' in poetry." However, I rather like concision & wordplay, which I guess is not dramaturgy. But I like to think of cleaning up one's art as drama-detergy. He also says, "The practice of an art should be immersed in the bringing-into-existence-as-creativity process. The *result* need *not* communicate." And it seems to me a subject should be written all about, but nothing particularly discursive should be said. Let a subject shimmer a bit, but stick your main point into the reader's head. Call it justifiable.

O, Let 'er Press

Art should be conditional,
i.e., conditions set by the
artist. Once set he should
not risk these conditions for
what is called "communication."

— Russell Atkins

O, let 'er press
the kiss of font
a tactile sense.

End season's start
rote a grave
aria
hosanna.

Butt tasteful tact
some wisdom is
— some *whiz* **dumb** *wasp* —

Tragicomedy's
Janus wits
as fall hiemal
spring estival.

Gong to the Well, but Hell

"The practice of an art should be immersed in the bring-ing-into-existence-as-creativity process. The *result* need *not* communicate."

— Russell Atkins

Per haps, *their* **his** ¿what whiz!
dumb one *cant* deposit.

Onion lay errs of mean-
ing may bring one . . . two . . . tears.

Indirect, a bank-shot,
combination **boggle**.

Enough! to make one sick
as what's swallowed they 'ate.

Per fact shun as **be** *lief*
the dew *con* **dense** often.

A greed, dough, **a** *leven* —
as what's **be** *lo,* vanish.

As wee *moo* **fin**, gasping . . .
Bull! *Bone china* shat**ters**.

& that's no valentine!
Though *thought*: Known, weave bean forked!!!

& a tiff a cult task
might be, braying . . . I dare.

Duck! The few chewers come,
be leave us in the lurch.

BAR

I was just minding my own business
which we might say is po' biz.
I cannot say I'm very certain
how seriously the world takes this.

An adjacent young woman adrift
in the milieu of her escort's distraction,
I in the company of a friend
my business was to run some poems by,

& at his instigation I tendered her
it seemed to the reception of some assent.
But propriety & territory
might a troglodyte invoke
where my intent was to be but sociable
my poetry won for me a mouse

whereupon he was ejected;
& Jim & I shared a couple gratis.

JOHN GABEL

Recollecting Russell Atkins

I met Russell Atkins in the 1970s. Cleveland, at that time, had barely emerged from one of the most painful eras in its modern history, a time of great racial turmoil followed by a growing awareness and embrace of the rights of its citizenry. A time ripe for looking inward, for self-expression, for a critical appraisal of institutions. In other words, a time for poetry! Poets from all over the city found themselves, organized one another, and began presenting readings and workshops in settings as various as churches, museums, schools, parks and, on one unforgettable occasion, in a junkyard. Many voices linger in memory: Cy Dostal, Barbara Angell, Daniel Thompson, Robert Wallace, and Alberta Turner, who are no longer with us. The poetry scene was scrappy and boisterous, and, if it had a calm center, it would be Russell Atkins. A child raised decently in a troubled time, a school boy encouraged to read and, ultimately, to write. He never succumbed to the pretensions of some of the era's louder voices. He was, to use his own words, "an outright man," a gifted and industrious craftsman, the friend and publisher of many poets. When I first heard Russell Atkins read his poetry, he already had a national following. I was a middle-aged actuary, and I had just begun to write poetry myself. His gift, his poise, his style in poetry *and* in demeanor registered deeply on me. We are now both old men. I write little nowadays, but I remember the heady days of Cleveland in the 70s and 80s when many men and women began to parse the world in love and anger, and we had always the exemplary presence of Russell Atkins at the center. And I am grateful.

Live Oak

"The live oak wants one hundred years to find its final form."

It seems little to ask
considering the decisions
about where to put out limbs
and how each branch should bend yet end
in satisfaction of the whole,
spreading fifty twister feet
in each direction a man might walk.

"And a hundred years to stand."

At evergreen attention,
limbs cantilevered fifty feet,
trailing Spanish moss and dropping
the leaves that age withers,
and an annual crop of acorns
to sleep in the shade and blacken
a circle of ground that remembers
no other purpose.

"And yet another to die."

Drooping elbows to the ground,
settling upon arbor or fence
gradually without an abrupt
giving way or breaking way.

The speaker, claiming eighty years,
had not seen the cycle
but was sure her family had,
neither giving way nor breaking way,
passing the oak from father to daughter.

Three hundred years to fountain up and out,

to pose ever green turning in the wind
repeating endless pattern,
a fountain rising and falling within,
dropping back to renew itself at root.

Outlasting the owner's deed
if not his fountain of blood,
itself rising and falling back,
renewing need and will

in the flow of generations.

The S.S. Meteor

In forward holds they sleep
In stacks five deep on canvas
Stretched on iron racks two feet
From cot to cot ten to top
A thousand men in each
Less those who would not sleep
For fear or stench or heat
Or overwhelming madness

Who choose instead to lie
The night on steel decks to watch
The strange southern sky unaware
Of the throbbing ship's gentle roll

Six thousand miles
Six waiting weeks
Saltwater showers
Two meager meals
To Leyte

Island by island

The morning deck is covered
Rail to rail with green fatigue
While the bow cleaves two
rolling waves
In relentless zigzag pattern

And she not meant for this
Labors heavily remembering
Other cargos other trips

There is something

About the way she sits in the water
The way she works up
Then slides down the horizon
From point to point slowly changing shape
Until she is finally only superstructure
And then drops off the end
Of sight   not of mind
There is something satisfying
About that out of sight shape
Going somewhere   going on

NORMAN JORDAN

Association with Russell Atkins

Norman Jordan, who died in 2015, became acquainted with Russell Atkins during the turbulent years of the Civil Rights Movement in Cleveland, Ohio. Russell's poetic genius and his input in the publication of *Free Lance* magazine was an inspiration and encouragement to Jordan's own creative expressions. They became friends and worked closely together organizing the Cleveland-based Muntu Poets. Russell also wrote the Introduction to Norman's second collection of poems entitled *Above Maya*. Having lost touch with Russell after moving from Cleveland, Norman was delighted when he, Russell, and other Muntu poets reconnected in 2013. And he was especially pleased to see the publication of a biography of Russell's life and work.

One Eyed Critics

3:30
In the morning
With not
A soul in sight
We sat
Four-deep at
A traffic light
Talking about how
Dumb and brainwashed
Some of our Brothers and Sisters are
While we waited
For a green light
To tell us
When to go.

I was Cool

I was cool
I was hip
Right down to my fingertips.

Then I fell in love.

FOR MY SONS: NEOGRIOTS

I am proud to be father of
21st century word-warriors and business men

Young men who have spent years turning life into music
Selling their product out of the trunks of their cars

Holding nine to fives flipping burgers
To buy bling and a tank of gas to get to the next gig

Wearing baggy low hanging Ethnic-made attention getting
fashions
Spitting shock & awe lyrics for their Black-owned companies

Between the lines protesting poverty & racism
And showing love for their generation

They are phoenixes rising out of the ashes
Of the Black Arts Movement.

Ode To My Sister Mittie

If
Yellow
Suns
Could
Talk

Rose
Red
Rocks
Would
Melt
Into

Blue
Moons

Souls
Of
The
Night
Raising
Art

Is
Love.

Mind and Soul After Dark

Naked
Scalding wet
From the sea
My soul stands wobbly
On its hind legs
The ghost of an exhausted poet
My mind, returning from the brink of surrender
Reaches out
For a formal position
Together, shaking the dust of a thousand deaths
Together, returning from a mad dream
Together, desperately trying to grasp and
Observe the last days of Spring

DIANE KENDIG

Still Wows Me

I first met Atkins in the mid-1970s while attending the C.S.U. poetry workshop in Cleveland. He barely spoke except on our rides home in Leonard Trawick's yellow VW Bug, or, later, in my old red Granada, and when he did, he just cracked me up with his acerbic humor and his breath-taking, right-on honesty. So I looked up and read *Here In The*, and there, too, I found him darkly funny, deeply observant, wonderfully quirky. After a decade, I had to leave Cleveland, and I lost track of Russell, as did my old friend in poetry Bob McDonough, one of Russell's biggest fans. Years later, together with Shaheed and Yaseen, we went looking for Russell and we found him, with the help of the Michael Dumanis and Kevin Prufer book, *Russell Atkins: On the Life and Work of an American Master*. Since then, we four have worked on several projects with Russell, who still makes me laugh, still wows me with his latest words.

VISITING RUSSELL WITH ALARM

A man shouted, "I'm here to get the body," as he came in the door with a gurney. The door alarm went off. Russell, whose room at The Grande Pavilion Nursing and Rehabilitation is just inside this door and this alarm, looked up, and said softly, "Oh no." Then Russell and I returned to our work, transcribing his new poem. But the alarm, which is piercing, did not stop. The man shrugged sheepishly and continued down the hall with his rattling cart. The alarm continued. It screeched on and on. I went and stood out in the hall looking desperate. An aide came into Russell's room, grabbed a long clamp for reaching things, and whapped the alarm with it. It stopped. Moments later, the man came back with the body on the gurney, which got stuck halfway out the door, setting the alarm off again. The man wheeled the body back in, closed the door, and started over, looking at us apologetically and shrugging again as the alarm went off for the third time. An aide shouted to him to lean on the alarm and the door at the same time. As these were over three feet apart, he stood puzzling that. Finally an employee arrived and leaned on the alarm while the gurney driver leaned on the door. The door opened, the alarm stopped, the body rolled out the door. Russell and I went back to work on his new poem, "Rest Home."

A Double Abecedarian for NaPoWrMo

All my poet friends and I are looking for pizazz
by working out at the pome machine each day,
counting or listing or otherwise composing, mumbling, "Lummox,
Dunderhead, dear me my pome machine seems broke, wow!"
Every idea I ever had seems, Luv,
fled from my brain, off in the bayou or, in a mumu,
getting on the bus without me, so abrupt,
hightailing away, the sonnets, haikus and glosas.
I need though, thirty days of this, altogether,
jump-starting my way from the ghazals of Iraq,
keeping at it through haiku, free verse, wishing for an APP
like those that exist for other tasks, arriving at last to mean."

MUSHFAKE

Mushfake (n.) - prison slang for objects made from scrap materials in the institution

In Edinburgh Castle, we lean over
the glass case of two hundred fifty year old
mushfake—what the modern prisoners call
these boxes, toys, and knick knacks ingeniously
jury-rigged and shaped and glued by inmates,
a making-do to make.

In Maine they sell a lot of mushfake from
a huge showroom floor, so much it's not exactly
mushfake, as the prison provides materials,
just as it did in Saugus, Massachusetts,
where seventeenth century Scottish prisoners
slaved at making English iron tools.

All this time, we're seeing, the practices continue,
yet we call them *practice*: mushfake, rulings,
bookings, torture--a U.S. Justice said today that it's not
punishment if the captive is not convicted of a crime;
we're just retrieving information, a ruling
I'd call mushfake, if it weren't so badly constructed.

THE FOREST ANIMALS' DIVERSIONS

after John Donoghue

My friend emails, "On Paxil, I miss
the intensity, feel a sort of flattening."
I fret about that flattening,
and I'm not taking Paxil,

never took anything even
back when everyone took everything.
There I was, without a face, a teeming,
a grimace of my own impulses

and poetry bundled them,
live wires off to spread messages
which had been scattered sound and images:
ducks lined up and sunned on a log

during a trip I never took out of the city.
A bear I never saw lumbered into town
and feasted on doughnuts that cops threw down
at him after he'd emptied all the bird feeders.

My friend is gone this weekend
building a second house in Vermont,
certain as several other poets that woods,
ocean, desert or prairie's where the poems are

though she snagged her last in Cambridge
at her friend's grave, where the red fox found her,
as in downtown Denver a red fox found my family
the Christmas after my sister died.

DAWN LUNDY MARTIN

On Russell Atkins

As Aldon Lynn Neilsen points out, critics tend to be short-sighted when considering the African-American literary tradition, often writing out of history those writers who don't already fit neatly into a mode, convention, or movement. Russell Atkins, for example, had long theorized and engaged in a kind of creative practice around deconstruction, long before deconstruction had entered the academy. One might argue that some of the theories and practices at work in Language poetry, as well, were anticipated in Russell Atkins's poems before Language poetry emerged. Yet, as the Language movement was narrated as predominantly white and male, questions about subject position and privilege continued to complicate the political aspirations of the Language poets and raise other questions about why poets of African American descent like Atkins have been narrated out of genealogies of postmodernism, experimentation, and innovation. I love Atkins because he is a key part of an historical trajectory of unconventional African American poetics that I find myself engaged in. Should we call like "kinship?" I like to think so.

From *Good Stock*

O, release, this rough
     rot—

to be born of Sarah's head, through
     sieve, seized wreckage,

our laboring hulk— age-old sag—

Scarf-wrapped faces.

     Quarry

        metal dust   beyond dark space

     is possible   tribe

     under stain, father's black tongue—

     Neck exposed toward sky,

     shins bubbling in heat—

is positioned for irretrievable

              loss, one in each archway

picturesque as summer—

     one layer gone, another absolute without—

the robberies—

Ibibio shrine. Ibibio man in a cowboy hat.

—the holding place—
on edge of continent—late day falls—gut
tumbling, night warm, welted warmth [We

      bracket infinity]

Stare through this window in

      my belly where my mother

left her good stock, her pertinent cells,

      her matter that matters—

Tiny particles forever floating—

What is more frightening than a black face
confronting your gaze from the display case?

ROBERT E. MCDONOUGH

Russell Atkins

Cyril A. Dostal once told me, "Russell Atkins has the best poetry head in Cleveland." More than forty years later, I'm still not sure what Cy meant by that, but I know what I mean. Russell has always regarded the work of art as a made object responsible primarily to the artist's satisfaction. The intelligence and extent of his means to achieve his own satisfaction have created a body of work that endures to give joy to the rest of us. He is a poet's poet (and editor, playwright, composer, and theorist.) I am still learning from him.

A FAVOR FOR ORPHEUS

(For R. A.)

Through a graveyard to a funeral home
is not a usual trip (most go the other way
once) but his true goal was the piano
he'd be allowed to use there. That permission
was an honor, he was given to feel,
along with pity and the calculation
of the value of gratitude from a man like him
with an old mother and aunt at home.

He felt he was bestowing an honor by using the piano
to pick out and put down a thicket of notes
worth his graveyard excursion, worth
anyone's finding a way through, but
failing the whistle test. No one—
not his Cleveland Orchestra friends
who would record it for him but hate it,
not any imaginable audience, not
the boxed dead all around him who'd surely
be willing to listen if they could come back for fifteen
more minutes—
no one would ever whistle it.

"A Good Drinker"

–Louise Mooney

I hope someone will call me that
when I'm dead, out of respect
for my respect. I hope they'll say,
"He never had a Singapore Sling or
a Fuzzy Navel, and he never tried to quit;
just beer and wine, a whiskey, showing up
every day, keeping in touch."
They might say, "Once he learned how
he didn't get drunk;
and even when he was young,
the only sign he was drunk
was that he acted sober."

2014

A woman who's leaving may still
share one last night.

This beautiful summer; ash aloft
from western fires cools us here in the east
most days, back to the normal
of an old man's youth, or below.
There is rain here, though none
where the fires are, and profuse green.
None of us are happy with our tomatoes.

When I was young I supposed the worst
of dying would be the thought
of all this glory going on without me.
Now the worst is
it won't.

High Summer

High summer, and tattoos bloom
up and down from blouses and shorts
of lithe young women, while just-as-young men,
who can't afford roses, dream of following tattoos
to ecstatic conclusions.

High summer, and roses bloom,
and old men
have them cut to take
to our just-right loves, who will bring
decades to bloom in our peaceful beds.

RAY MCNIECE

A Multifaceted Aesthetic

A reclusive fellow on the periphery of Cleveland poetry, Russell Atkins was first recommended to me by my mentors in the Poets' League. But I could find few poems. Finally, I found some in two national and local anthologies, and when I did, the lines, even on the yellowed, musty pages, still shimmered. That is his magic. To call him a poet's poet is an understatement. What attracted me, and permeated my consciousness, was the seamless synesthesia of his verses; they are musical sketches, pictorial sound-scapes.

The juxtaposition of conjunctions, the nouns and adjectives energized into verbs, are created not for the pyrotechnical effects, but are the form following function. And the very city of Cleveland pulses through his linguistic DNA. His poetry flows from a multifaceted aesthetic which "summoned ascends huged up// then softs."

Boneyard Breathing

The way to the other world
looks the same as the way here—
zazen all vison,
sunset flaking shadow dry rot red paint wood facade
of the shed on the edge of the boneyard,
breathing wider the forlorn 'hood that surrounds the dead,
where the birds are bullets whizzing over bare heads,
breathing beyond the wild blue yonder redtail hawk circles,
plummeting beak scree strike, talon pierce, the rabbit's
field of vision blacks out,
curling up in the weeds, uncurling worms squirming,
ending deep in dark matter mother again,
breathing womb of breath, womb of death,
tomb of flesh, the only home we'll ever own,
breathing awake, asleep, awake, asleep,
generations come and gone,
breathing skull on headstone
orange lichens awake.

Skull Relief

650-950 Meso America
Cleveland Museum of Art

A skull is a skull is a skull, that same smile
sculpted limestone from a Mayan temple,
arm femurs upraised, finger bones splayed
welcoming the arrow-tongued vulture --
even skeletons are devoured eventually, leaving
only stone socket stare rekindling brain's colors.
How empty the body will be but for that weight.
Look upon this and weep salty, paltry tears,
rain etching gutters down its gritted face.
Pre-Vera Cruz Mayans gazed on this familiar,
carved from daily beheading festivities,
bodies kicked heartless down pyramid stairs.

Here the skull sits now on white pedestal
perused by viewers in museum going apparel,
uncomfortable shoes shifting over wood floor.
PLEASE DO NOT TOUCH in Bold block letters.
The column's reverse depicts chieftain warrior,
fierce teeth, brandishing a long feathered spear --
the hand that held it long gone, and the hand
that hued it, as are hands that traced the skull,
relieved it was not their own or those they loved.
And what of the hands that hoisted this shard?
Rubbing my lower back, I walk past the guard,
through the skull of the museum into the light.

Drips

Cold bowl of oatmeal stares
back, 7:15 again.
Grey clouds hang
like wet newspaper.

I drive to work past the dead
deer, same as yesterday.
Cornfield furrows seep
late winter snowmelt.

At my white cubicle, first thing,
I water the lone plant, a gift,
leaves more grey than green.
It's not flourishing. It's not wilting.

Muzak mumbles, the same
songs rotate five times a day.
I want to scream death
metal. I mute.

Ceiling light globe hangs
above boss's office, dusty sun
that never sets.
I turn on the screen.

Columns of numbers march,
exiles across Siberian tundra.
I fill hours with them.
Coffee machine drips bitter sizzle.

JOAN NICHOLL

Poet and Friend

Russell Atkins, poet and friend. We value his criticism and his company. Those of us who have had the opportunity to rescue Russell from the perils of public transportation after some workshop or reading have had the added enjoyment of good conversation and gentle humor on the drive to his house. We read together, Russell and I, along with Cy Dostal and Chris Franke at the Harbor Inn in The Flats back in the Seventies. What a mixed bag that must have been! He was such a story teller. I remember his tale about how it rained in his living room. Any householder could identify with his distress and his embellishing humor in his telling of it. And now we are the elder statesmen. It's good to be together again.

SPACES

Some things you learn slowly
once, in Vermont
snow fell in the night
settled on cows, covering their markings
they huddled in pastures
ankles in mud
chewing grass
breath and dung steaming

I thought, they are one thing
snow, cows, mud, grass, dung
also, much later, a tree
like a blade of grass
is not to be considered separately

sometimes walking in the woods with my dog
rain or snow
in my hair, her fur
it is not quite clear where I leave off
and she and the earth begin

families are like that
separated, only others see empty spaces

Reflection

At dusk
when street lights come on
ghosts appear
in a row beside the bed, watching.

Paler shapes come
preceded by whispers
pass through them
like wind
blowing through stones.
Sometimes they merge
float together, suspended
then disappear in the fireplace
or down the hall.

At last
they leave my ghosts
to keep their watch alone, baleful
and growing weak
as dawn presses
their shoulders to the wall.

people who write about fishing

Carver, MacLean, they fascinate me
Bishop, a woman, fished
and got a fine poem
a sport I know nothing about

but I like to swim in ponds
small lakes
feel water plants
gently grasping

soft mud
small rough nibbles on my ankles
like a cat's tongue
fish are curious

warm golden places
cool dim green
moving through changing light
swimming a painting

what do fish know of beauty
in themselves dark flickers
or in what they see
a dragon fly could be dinner

to be in there with them
to have them on the plate
it's the part in the middle
I know nothing about

MWATABU OKANTAH

On Russell

To this day, I am not sure just how or when I first met Russell Atkins. I do know the CSU Poetry Center's Leonard Trawick introduced me to his work. I remember being struck by the title of the collection of poems Leonard had given me to read—*Here in The*. Sometime later, historian James G. Spady came to Cleveland doing research on Marcus Garvey. Driving Spady to the Western Reserve Historical Society one afternoon, he changed subjects on me and asked if the poet Russell Atkins still lived in Cleveland. My old Director at CSU, Curtis Wilson, gave us Russell's home address. It was Spady who made me aware of the underground importance of Russell's work. I am one of those poets that does not read a lot of poetry. I loved reading Russell's work because it was so unlike anything else I read. I think I was drawn to his poetry precisely because I could never describe it beyond its private power.

More than his work, however, I was most touched by Russell's gentle yet resolute spirit. Looking back on that day, we had a difficult time trying to find his house. He lived on a street that was broken up into disjointed sections. At one point, we stopped at what appeared to be a dead end, looked at each other and laughed, "Here in The." Sitting in his cluttered living room, I felt privileged to be allowed into this reclusive creative artist's world. My experience with Russell taught me to just be who I am and to find my own distinct voice in my art. Comfortable in his own aesthetic skin, Russell taught me to trust my own style and just sing free.

there is a power

Lift Every Voice…
and if we could
would we sing? would we
sing guttural black
notes? would we
sing auction block cries from twisted
slave mother lips
in agony
fighting to hold onto her
sold down-river child?

… Nat Turner saw visions in the sky
but there was no pollution
then:

Gladys Knight also sang *A Rainy*
Night in Georgia,
but rainy nights do not always follow
lynched visions
in this still barren land—it rained that night Nat's
white hooded black angels
stood standing …
"lift every voice …"
and if we could
would we
sing?

"Unforgivable Blackness"

the more things change
the more
things stay the same:

they looked at us
and called him "the black menace."
Jack Johnson was the embodiment of their
worst whitemare—
a black man who dared
to be free.
a black man who could see,
who saw himself black,
saw himself bold, saw himself beautiful and
stubborn, swimming
through white foaming
rapids, battling against raging racist currents,
jumping relentless roaring waters into
a calm but shark infested sea.

if *they* only knew.
they do not know how
to know.
do not want to know—
they destroyed *Black Wall Street* in Tulsa.
THEY let *THE MOVE FIRE*
burn in Philly—
("grab on to whatever is left …")
random-white-men lynched James Byrd in Jasper.
stand-your-ground lynched Trayvon Martin in Sanford.
police lynched Michael Brown in Ferguson.
black-story-well says
another one of us is always next.

broken memories. broken dreams.
wandering visions.
wondering thoughts.
remembering who we were—
who we have become?

ugly in our beauty. brutal in our love.
seductive in our poison.
radioactive to the touch.

unforgivable blackness:

primordial blackness.
blackness so black so bright
so, "this little light of mine,
i'm gonna make it shine"
blackness,

still shining in us
for reasons
even we
fail to understand ...

          for Jack Johnson
          (1878-1946)

NATHAN OLIVER

Russell Atkins

He was/is the coryphaeus of Avant guard composition and experimental poetry in Cleveland. His oeuvre, amazingly striking and varied, destined Russell Atkins as a source of inspiration for many wide-eyed, pencil-ready, aspiring poets and town criers. He was my go-to source for the Cleveland literati and beyond. He was for me a wonder of staccato, rumpled, fluffy, fastidious pronouncements generously shared with a nudge or two. In 1988 he was the subject of the Chesnutt Record, a publication of the Chesnutt Literary Society where he was honored for his contributions to the Literary Arts. I am delighted now to join in this tribute to my friend and unwitting mentor. May the Ancestors continue to smile on him.

For Russell Atkins

eye remember W i n d
the sOn was **high** over Cleve land
                    n
                u
Spot would r   like a magnificant
                    lancefreenthe   win
The f
      a
        l
        l
          en leaves wood Russ   ell
   under foot of time and WEIGHT and
Con   cret cracked open
         still in time the wet dripped
Thru **GRAND** streets forced to guess
at their fate
                      r
            u   n
     then t   ed back to the ground
                                    to embrace
many   L   O   N   G
                        hidden roots

For Nelson, While Remembering Ruby Dee's "My Last Good Nerve"

He is the sprouts of spring, the restless winter wind, the brisk hurried steps of fall, and the warmth of storms beating down upon the land of histories and mysteries interrupted by ambition that should never tame itself.

He is a dragon-slayer, a mountain-climber, and has been spotted occasionally walking the water of rivers ancient and deep as Langston's dreams

His nascent vision forged out of self-doubt will never rule his brighter moments.
He must learn to bathe in the Holy Water of Self-Acceptance and Love, which overflows to drown all chariots of pursuit across the Red Seas of America's landscape

He is our hope, he is our reward, and he is our child of all his makings and marks boldly inscribed upon the heart of young intent looking for content.

He is my Son of Suns and the morning air for life to continue to flow past all graves of time and trouble. He is a young Turtle sticking out his neck and moving into his tomorrows.
I salute you my son, may the Creator grant you the victory.

Soyinka

3:15 AM train whistle challenging the night as it rumbles out of the East over J&L Steel tracks forged in the Flats of Cleveland.

I have greeted my cerebral visitor, Soyinka, with all fair fitting honored guests of sleepless nights
 "The mind" is indeed "its own place" and commanded to rest, resist as a freedom fighter declaring independence finding its own voice over my pitiful objections

Think of the wisdom of this tool that assigned a curiosity proclaims the right to work whatever shift it chooses even as it moves out of the way of oncoming trains rumbling down invasive tracks made in the USA by 2ND generation immigrant labor

It is spring '09', trout season: marred by wet, cold, damp, windblown weather that discounts my passion

The tracks, ¾ of a mile away, shuttle the train through my bedroom with urgency and a physics that I would have to Google if it really mattered in the scheme of things

Perhaps I could ask Soyinka the next time he keeps me up, wakes me up, greets me at the door of consciousness with the King's 'spotless black stallion' that I wish not to ride

Soyinka, Soyinka, Soyinka who has authorized you to bring this burden, this animal, this penciled train driven horse into my bedroom without a name to be announced and who does he seek in his death ride to the Great King?

Have I been invited even in the chaos of cosmic confusion when duty has been left undone?

Give me the sleep that ends as morning invites us to wake from regenerative slumber to beat the rain soaked earth even as the mud squishes between toes and mud pies await our judgment.

CARYL PAGEL

Note on Atkins

Here In The, published by the Cleveland State University Poetry Center in 1976, is a singular lyric record of Cleveland's sensual and sonic landscapes replete with surprising descriptions ("someplace in a disaster of grass"), imagistic twists ("like a top hat up/ sat down on"), and rhythmic trills ("into the mm wind/ rain now and again/ the mm wind") that mesmerize. It's clear in every line that Atkins is both a musician and an investigator of his home's ever-shifting energies. As a recent resident of Cleveland, I can attest to the profound influence of Atkins' work on this city (and beyond's) verse-loving inhabitants. Russell Atkins is one of the indisputable heroes of Cleveland's innovative literary history.

Telephone

There was fear involved—yes—some
fear and hesitancy to discuss what
you knew you had done but
had not yet told anyone   It
was nothing   You discussed it for
hours—all that nothing and what
nothing meant—what a shame it
would be to allow the nothing
to decay—to fade and fly
and die like all those nothings
that you both had had before
It felt like a new nothing
but you knew—instinctually—in your
frantic animal soul—that all nothing
sustains itself the same way—by
expanding—cracking—swallowing itself and all
around it—by colliding with old
nothings   You knew and discussed what
a nothing all your nothing was—
and yet you could not find
an end to it   This kind of
nothing kept going   It kept going
into itself and back out again
around the day—winding itself through
you and whispering things concerning you
across the wire and in sleep's
abysmal strangle and after all that
talk you felt true   Like a
new version of yourself you never

knew   A version of the very
dreadful nothing that you had always
had a vision of yourself becoming

Rumors

You are telling the story   You
are telling the story again   Twice
told you tell him the story
someone he knows told you   You
know the same someone the same
story but different aspects and facets
You were not present in this
story but in one story he
was and it was told to
you by someone you both know
You tell him another story about
himself that even he didn't know—
but you knew   You've known about
his story for quite some time
without knowing him and he knows
you   He recalls when you first
told a story—not the one
you are telling right now but
still true   You keep telling   You
want to keep telling him and
so you do and he does
too and at first you are

standing in the same place not
telling the story—just clues—because
you knew that you were going
to tell this story and it alarms
you that you knew   Your
sudden sentence is closing the room
He is telling a story that
is oddly similar to the story
told by you   It might be
a part of the same story—
a larger story—larger than you
or your telling of the story
or his telling it back to
you anew   But by now there
is just one story with two
tellers and it endures through both
the telling and the endless loop
that continues with or without you

KEVIN PRUFER

<u>Walking Down Euclid Avenue</u>

Five years ago, Michael Dumanis, then the director of the Cleveland State University Poetry Center, gave me one of the last available copies of Russell's *Here In The*. I remember it well: a hot and cloudless day in Cleveland, and I read that book walking down Euclid Avenue, astonished by poems that were utterly unlike anything I'd encountered before. They seemed so fresh, musically dexterous, witty, utterly original. Michael and I would go on to immerse ourselves in Russell's work and eventually edit a volume of poems and essays devoted to him. But, along the way, the great joy has been finding not only his writing, but Russell himself. He has, I learned, many of the qualities of his own poems—soft spoken, wry, observant, fiercely intelligent, and fun. My only wish is that I hadn't waited so long to discover him or his work.

In the Wheat Field

"It's your rabbit," the officer told the soldier
who pointed his rifle at the fleeing enemy
child.   The child was quick in the wheat,
so it took three shots before he tumbled
into the afterlife. Many years later
I put down my book about the war
and walk under the oaks' black branches
to where the snow has capped all the cars
in the elementary school parking lot.
The rooftops glitter meanly.
I have never killed anything and
look at me. I am like the boss of hell.
In the silent movie, the moon
took a rocket to the face and never
stopped smiling. Tonight its ashes
scatter over the rooftops. No, that's snow.
Of all the people he murdered,
that soldier could not forget how
the child swayed a moment in the wheat
before disappearing under the sea of it.
I once found a bullet casing right here
on this sidewalk and, not far from it,
a stain. How could I not imagine
the rest of that story? The cars
grow cool and dire in the parking lot,
and the sodium lights hum like enormous
insects. The soldier wrote a whole book about
what he had done, but it didn't help.
Come on and snow all over me,
come on and shower me with ash.
The sky is bone. The moon is a hole
in somebody's skull.

Menhirs

I was lying on the couch
and outside rain kept falling
so I turned the page of my magazine
while Mary hummed in the bedroom,
changing the sheets.
On television, a man went on about
dead empires. What was he saying?
Piles of stones, long stone walls
winding through the green fields of,
I guessed England, then
several mysterious stone circles
in the center of which were—
I knew what they were called—
menhirs. The television was
muted and the man moved his lips
again, perfectly comfortable
among the stones and wind,
in his tweed jacket, his bright red tie.
Mary was still humming,
pushing the beds back into place.
Once again, the sheets were
clean and smelled of soap.
Outside, the rain came down
in vast populations and now
I was slipping into sleep,
raindrops exploding on the windows,
wind leaning into the walls. That week,
a young woman I knew slightly
had drowned. They'd towed her empty boat
through the storm. I must write her family,
I thought from far away. Then, a sense,
like a warm wind, settled against me:
we drift through time
the way trees drift through rain.
We hold none of it. We hold
none of it. I felt terrified
in the bright room. On TV,

the man was still talking.
Mary pointed the remote control at him
as if to change the channel.
For a moment longer
menhirs glowed in the sunset.

P. K. SAHA

A Magnificent Reader

Back in the 1960's and 1970's Russell and I appeared before numerous audiences in the Cleveland area and read many poems, our own as well as famous poems by others. Russell was always a magnificent reader who captivated the audience with the rise and fall of his cadences. I felt I could listen to him for hours.

Blue Whales

Colossal cucumbers with flippers, tails,
massive mammal hearts, heaving, gliding
troubadours of the deep,
chanting spells from ocean rim to rim,
luring our souls into cold depths
where language turns numb in dark dreams,
quickening small mammal hearts.

Language Lessons

The day I saw departure in your eyes,
I enrolled in a Berlitz course
to learn the language of loss.

The pronouns are simple,
but the verbs of existence
are all irregular and hard to learn.

Cut

Our words didn't cut deep
but they were
hard as a glass-cutter.
One light tap now...

The Trap

Everything was so quiet, moist, and inviting
I simply had to enter.
And the heavy door that snapped shut
was well concealed by your arms
stretched out like leafy branches.

Well, I admit I was taken in,
but for some years now I have been checking
a couple of hinges
that are getting rusty
and might just snap, if I use all my strength.

Ghosts at the Taj

Resting by the pool late in the day,
we look up at the dazzle of white
marble: the huge central dome
reigning over lesser domes, walls,
niches, arches, arabesques,
and the four slender minarets.

In all that symmetry against the sky,
nothing is unplanned. The inscriptions
at great heights are graduated to appear
uniform to eyes at ground level.
The cypress trees and the water
are the image of Paradise.

Inside, on the queen's cenotaph,
what seem to be painted flowers
are patterns of coral and gemstones:
carnelian, jasper, jade, moonstone,
and lapis lazuli. Twenty thousand men

toiled over twenty years.

No one knows their names,
the names of all those men
who shaped the marble,
set stones in inlaid patterns,
dug the reflecting pools
and lined them with cypress trees.

The emperor hired workers
from near and far, perhaps even
craftsmen from Instanbul and Venice.
Where are their names?
Inscriptions merited graduated letters,
but the artists' names were never recorded.

The breeze picks up, stirring the water,
and the ripples flow from right to left:
Urdu writing! Names in liquid letters:
Anwar Din... Ali Ahmed...
Raj Singh... Amjad Khan...
Paolo Ricci... Narayan Lal...

For the emperor, they were hired hands,
not in the ranks that merited glory
in golden calligraphy on pages of history.
The one name he glorified was the queen's.
Now the sighs of ghosts in cypress trees
barely stir the silvery surface of the pool.

M.A. SHAHEED

An Inspiration for Me

I met Russell in 1966 as a member of the Muntu Poets workshop. He was a different kind of guy than I was used to dealing with. He spoke proper English, wore round glasses and a sport jacket. Of course I was only mid-twenties at the time. After a while I began to appreciate the things he taught. I could see that I had more in common with him than I thought at first. At some point he became an inspiration for me. His style was different in the way he presented things. I still visit with him often and continue to be even more impressed with him. Russell was a forerunner and I'm happy to have known him as a young man and as an older man. It's honor to be in another anthology with him after many years.

Thoughts While Drinking Yohimbe

A combination of sounds turns my words
around and makes them flow with ease.

They seem to blend with wind gusts that
carry them to their destinations.

Coffee cups filled to the brim. Pens running
running out of ink.

Words drop like brain rain. Logic impaled on
mistakes geniuses made.

Someone floundering on someone's... Why?
The rogue is in vogue.

Overpaying for trash while animation is
suspended. Saying screw you is now an art form.

Ponder

My head can no longer hold
secret sounds that escape
through my ears. They leak. They
speak to unfamiliar themes that
see ghosts. They are caught in the
rhythm and can't get away. All
this exists between the clouds
and the higher skies. This I see.

Below, snow flakes cake sidewalks.
Below, fetid winds blow dirt past
dust pans. Baby Grands are played
 by those who can play them. When
the sounds change pace I race to catch
up. I want to see the pinnacle
when I reach it.

[LISTENING]

The sounds get under my skin again and
make me smile, reducing my need
for music.

I love the sounds of paper bags as they
crumple
 in my hands.

I like to hear the light switch click.
The mousetrap's snap! They make me smile
Once more.

I heard some sounds late one night I couldn't
identify. When I woke I realized it was smoke
racing up the chimney walls.

I love the sounds of chiming bells
tangled in my
hair.

The steps of the boogie man as he
closes the back
 door.

I love the sound of falling branches
 from the leaves of palm
trees.

I like the sound of my pen against
 my glass desktop.

I like the screams of dying rats.
The sound of my knife as it cuts my cantaloupe.

The sound of boiling water as it over f
lows the
 kettle.

I love the sounds of satisfaction when
flying my paper
 planes.

I enjoy the sound of the rain, of the train as it
rattles along jointed rail.

I find benefit in the sounds of healing of
feeling inspiration coursing through my
veins.

I love the sounds of depth.

I love the sounds of the sounds that surround me.

I liked the way love sounded when I fell in it.

JOHN STICKNEY

A Quiet Soft-spoken Presence

Poets are rarely forgotten; to start with they are rarely remembered. Russell Atkins remains one of the exceptions. As a newbie poet, I regularly attended two monthly poetry workshops, sponsored by the CSU Poetry Center and by the Poets League of Greater Cleveland. Mixed among the bombast, there was a quiet, soft-spoken presence at those workshops. When he spoke, real poets paid attention. Who was this guy? I remember going to the library, reading Russell's poems in collections, anthologies and in copies of his magazine Free Lance. When I was lucky enough to drive Russell from the workshops to his home on Grand Ave., we would discuss poetry and his methods of composing. Those small conversations, his comments on any of the workshop poems, gave me a real sense of how to reveal the value of words. If all art aspires toward the condition of music, does it not follow that music aspires to the condition of Russell Atkins' poetry?

Poem in Three Parts for Russell

When
Back in the day
We relied
On three-fold maps
For the
How to get
To the where
We wanted
Russell was the voice
Of our GPS

***

I think it was Bob or
Maybe John or Joan
But not Diane
Maybe Cy
Probably Cy
Who said Poets are
The utility infielders
Of literature
Sitting
There on the bench
Waiting to be called

The exception?
 Russell Atkins
Batting clean-up
Among this crew
Of good glove and no stick
The banjo hitters destined
For fungo duty in the
Minor leagues
The Punch and Judy's
The masters of looking
Bat resting

At the called third strike
RA hit the ball
It would sing
Like a poem
Sing

***

There in the

There in the poem There in the inherent mystery There in the same time and same place There in the new object set in the once new world There in the nobility of what we call text There in the open mouth in the closed mouth and in the air shaped sound There in the this of the that in what we say There in the nightly train yard There in the distant church bells reminder There in the chrome plated Hard Bargain Credit Union There in the resolute inaction in the doing and in the done There in the asking and the asked There in the true names of places There in the tendril streets of this town There in the space beside the cup There in the footnotes of syntax There in the endless laps of Earth There in the clouded past of present tense words There in the storefront words taken and words left There in the faux syllabus There in the stars made of woven music There in the making of puppets There in the evidence drawer in the moon coroner's office There in the palmistry pocket of that man's coat There in the pane of the broken window There in the weave of the scarf There in the good light of these shipsunk rooms There in the habit of words placed in the sticky terrain of the heart of the mouth of the ear There in the inkling of Armageddon the holy trigger and the unholy target There in the lattice of the real and the arbitrary There in the possibility of possibility There in the where we take a seat and in the there where we listen

Notes To "Poem in Three Parts for Russell":

Part One – Refolded three-fold road maps, like dogs, are random

Part Two - For Russell Atkins, Robert McDonough, John Donoghue, Diane Kendig, Joan Nicholl, Leonard Trawick, Cyril Dostal and all the rest who showed up armed with ten to fifteen copies on a Friday night.

Part Three – After Russell's collection *Here in The*

Against Flowering

I do not flower! I refuse to flower! Your elbows are like green stuttering

pebbles, recently crawling across uneven surfaces. Your lips, a ruined tin of potted meat.

See. How do you feel when your body is treated as a few lines and then
later another adjective...turned into a few lines and later another
adverb... Immortal?

I think not.

The Best Location

The houses of our city are tall and beautiful. Our shoes are black and our gloves are brown. Buttons are large and easily persuaded. We keep the Devil in a refrigerator. The cool air lessens his power, sugars his disposition and allows us to determine if the light stays on when the door is closed. Though, admittedly, one day he says yes, the very next, no. Statisticians are busy tallying and analyzing. Soon all mysteries will be solved. And the houses of our city are beautiful and tall.

KENT TAYLOR

Russell Was Key

I first met Russell in early 1963, after discovering a copy of *Free Lance* at Publix Book Mart. He and his aunt kindly greeted me at their home on Grand Avenue, where Russell showed me the model train layout his uncle had built in the basement. Russell urged me to attend the next meeting of the Free Lance workshop, where I met d.a.levy and Adelaide Simon. Russell published me in several issues of *Free Lance* magazine. I also participated with Russell in three seminars at the Phillis Wheatley Association, as well as poetry readings.

So Russell was key to my development as a writer in Cleveland's exploding poetry scene. He may be the wisest human I've ever met.

For Russell Atkins

to be
in the moment
means being
no more
than next
to nothing

Chasing Helen

I measure morphine
        and Dilaudid
      and hope
      greed makes cancer
          careless enough
        to drop the leash
        that pulls you away

you get lost
        without moving
  as the labyrinth
   shifts
inside your head
   breaking the thread
of my touch

you've become
      unbearably beautiful
  but like a bird
      crossing the sun
    blinding
    to follow

12-29-68 CLEVELAND

the night
   of winter
  clings to this city
like fingers frozen to steel

   the freeway spills
headlights from a lost
      football championship
and we grow
under the loss
     and gain something
    unknown to winners

the ugliness of an industrial
     winter surrounds
as steel mills turn snow
    black and unmeltable

my eyes die
every mile
in this palpable dark

 my arms wither
   in the lake's
    wind of ice
til march

   april
       may warm
   in a flush of green
      and sun
   bring something back
unseen
but remembered

the veils fall
we walk and laugh
   like california will never
      know

HARBOR INN BLUES

out of work
    family broken past repair
       idle days
wandering the city
visiting jim lowell to talk
    of books and misery
      then descending
to the Harbor Inn
   for a little drinking
   like we have for
       five years

the bar nearly empty
    in the afternoon
  free of the suburban slummers
    that nightly clog
  the flat's twisted depths
there
     beneath huge bridge spans
      that sing
          as trucks speed overhead
    we nurse obscure spirits

     before leaving maybe a
  free one from mike
      along with a joke

then home
         east for jim
   me westward

LEONARD TRAWICK

A Fierce Devotion to His Arts

When I got to know Russell in the 70s, I came to admire
him for several apparently incompatible qualities. He nev-
er vaunted his many talents and accomplishments, but
always seemed modest and self-deprecating. At the same
time, from his good nature and sly humor one could tell
that he was comfortable with himself and the world. On
the other hand, I gradually realized that this seemingly
easy-going fellow had a fierce devotion to his arts, both
musical and literary. I can think of few artists who have
given themselves so fully and so successfully to the devel-
opment of their talent. And, though Russell's poems often
have a layer of humor, there is also often a grim undercur-
rent revealing his awareness of the full spectrum of human
experience.

Entropic

You might as well accept it—there's no way
to beat the cosmic system; all things must
submit to the great process of decay.

You want the pictures of your life to stay
unfaded, never crumbling into dust?
You might as well accept it: there's no way.

Your plumbing springs a new leak every day—
so what? You ought to know bad pipes are just
work of that old world-processor, decay.

Sooner or later your new Chevrolet
will stall and sink to its eternal rust—
you might as well accept it. There's no way,

either, to keep old age's ills at bay:
you feel twinges of joints but none of lust?
Simply the normal process of decay.

No one's exempt from it, and who can say
that what is universal is unjust?
And yet . . . oh, hell, accept it. There's no way
to halt the grand procession of decay.

Ship-Shape

Whatever power gives us ship-shape things—
spit shines, blue jays, the shut of straight-hung doors,
sleek tongue-in-grooves that spear from April bulbs,
sentences that, after they've wandered through
a maze of clauses, teetering on the brink
of syntax, click together in the nick
of a completing verb—this power I praise.

Praise too for all the things that can be fixed—
our rewired lamp, my brother's retooled valves,
cruel words I was permitted to retract.
As for botched things and things beyond repair,
I praise the slow power that levels earth
and makes even for them a tabernacle,
their place among the ship-shape daffodils.

Ode to Grits

Not gritty, but grist—
character from rough milling,
stripped of harshness
by a mess of potash—

this *tabula rasa* of the table,
soft cement of menus,
brings out everyone's best:
no wonder it's called *harmony*.

A fried egg cringes
on a bare hard plate,
but on this white divan
it lounges like an odalisque.

Those burly bumpkins,
country ham and redeye,
in its tasteful hands turn
to banquet Beau Brummells.

Launching pad for salsa,
cheddar's pillow: without it,
oh beef where is thy tang,
oh gravy, thy victualry?

Butter gilds this lily,
but woe to the wretches
who stoop to the adultery
of sugar and cream:

may their sausages
languish on Wonderbread;
may they drink only warm Bud Lite
and watch Lawrence Welk reruns forever.

LEWIS TURCO

Fast Friends

When I founded the Cleveland Poetry Center at Fenn College in the early sixties, Russell Atkins was an early and regular participant in the programs and Forums. That was when we became fast friends, and we've been friends and correspondents ever since. Our letters can be found in the Lewis Turco archive of Cleveland State University's Special Collections. I am delighted to be included in this birthday anthology. Gala Ninetieth Natal Anniversary, Russell!

AN ORDINARY EVENING IN CLEVELAND

I

Just so it goes: the day, the night—
what have you. There is no one on TV;
shadows in the tube, in the street.
In the telephone there are echoes and mumblir.gs,
the buzz of hours failing thru wires.

And hollow socks stumbling across
The ceiling send plaster dust sifting down
hourglass walls. Felix the cat has
been drawn on retinas with a pencil of light.
I wait grey, small in my cranny,

for the cardboard tiger on the
kitchen table to snap me, shredded, from
the bowl.

II

Over the trestle go
the steel beetles grappled tooth-and-tail — over and
over and over there smokestacks

lung tall hawkers into the sky's
spittoon. The street has a black tongue: do you
hear him, Mistress Alley, wooing
you with stones? There are phantoms in that roof's
trousers;
they kick the wind. The moon, on a

ladder, is directing traffic
now. You can hardly hear his whistle. The
oculist's jeep wears horn rim wind
shields; the motor wears wires on its overhead valves —

grow weary, weary, sad siren,

you old whore. It's time to retire.

III

The wail of the child in the next room quails
like a silverfish caught in a
thread. It is quiet now. The child's sigh rises to
flap with a cormorant's grace through

the limbo of one lamp and a
slide-viewer in your fingers: I cannot
get thin enough for light to shine
my color in your eyes; there is no frame but this for
the gathering of the clan. Words

will stale the air. Come, gather up
our voices in the silent butler and
pour them into the ashcan of
love. Look, my nostrils are dual flues; my ears are
the city dump; my eyes are the

very soul of trash; my bitter
tongue tastes like gasoline in a ragged
alley.

IV

The child cries again. Sounds
rise by the riverflats like smoke or mist in time's
bayou. We are sewn within seines

of our own being, thrown into
menaces floating in shadows, taken
without volition like silver
fish in an undertow down the river, down time
and smoggy evenings.

V

The child cries.

VI

Do you hear the voice made of wire?
Do you hear the child swallowed by carpets,
the alley eating the city,
rustling newsprint in the street begging moonlight with
a tin cup and a blindman's cane?

VII

The lamps are rheumy in these tar
avenues. Can you sense the droppings of
flesh falling between walls falling,
the burrowings of nerves in a cupboard of cars?
Can you hear the roar of the mouse?

VIII

There is nothing but the doorway
sighing; here there is nothing but the wind
swinging on its hinges, a fly
dusty with silence and the house on its back buzzing
with chimneys, walking on the sky

like a blind man eating fish in an empty room.

RA WASHINGTON

The Ultimate Astro-BLK

For me, it began as just a whisper, this name—"Russell Atkins". The whisper would occur when I was looking for examples of the avant-garde, or the beats, or . . . In Cleveland there were very few black writers you could meet, mostly the local scene consisted of good natured white boys, a few feminist women poets, and a few of the really boring language poets. That was what would bubble up from the surface, but if you dug deeper, if you hunted for the true artifacts or met just the right public intellectual—that whisper would happen. The poems of Mr. Atkins should be celebrated for their density of spirit, their formal inventiveness and the clarity of personhood in which they were birthed. It is one of the greatest art crimes of the past century. The fact that Russell Atkins existed saved my life. It showed me that I could inhabit any space, any modality and just be me. Atkins is the ultimate Astro-BLK, his line is the North Star for me and mines. VIVA!

SIBLING FACING

cuts
knowing you
given no in malice.
no evil, just the simple truth of it. the it signify. the life yours,
this time.

we can discuss the distinction but you will not like the answer
the story of ours,
you fail, and I watch, always the voyeur. so actor, I
we catch each others eyes and know what we've done.

knowing builds
the pressure, the failing
faces melt, disappear in revision. the lovers change
so we laugh [cuz] it's always US. brother locked.
history. the trauma genetic memory chokes;

we. are the Failing Things.

Lament.

My brother calls me the good one.
It's our joke. well his, of course.
I go along with it.
he does not call often.

There is a breaking point with siblings
that comes from time, the ticks ours
what is read in the hands.
the six years between us, our mother's womb
shortens every spring.

His children grow older
I have not met all of them
there are none for me.
I am the uncle, over there. tucked
along the cracks in voice.

the sound of his father, the jailor
with slighted shoulders
my brother has torture
in his throat.

Choirsong

The poet is wanted dead
Sweet the bounty.
Kill him pride.
Kill 'em pride.
It is the motioning of all dreams

That fuel a life.
You know this, yet you despise the dreamer?
Ponder me knuckle to cheek or knife to throat.
Gun trained on me, but false idols hold no worry.
You wish a master, yes. You wish a scapegoat.

So you wick on the willful, and snuff candle mist.
(plain speak)
The poet is wanted dead for bounty.

Ahh, call the poet, dead for chasing bounty
Wooooo. That dead word (don't say it),
Will for the former poet, here -
Take these pages, and call my name forever
At five, these places held no large thing.
He is, and will always be alive it seems
The type is magic, begot the ancient line gleams
Remember when it fell silent.
The listless or the list.
These are the ones we will acknowledge
These are the ones we will save.
All the lines are a jumble
Give finger to it all
Will never stop them poems from flowing
You, yes you.
Will have to kill us all.
For the poet is wanted for singing.
Yea, the poet is a want with singing,
And the choir is alive, and well.

118

MARY WEEMS

Black Genius-Poet

A few months ago, I had the honor of participating in a poetry event to celebrate the work and life of Black genius-poet Russell Atkins, the first African American, according to Nielsen in Black Chant, to "pursue such [experimental poetics] techniques as concretism and sound texts," and the inventor of psychovisualism. I decided to select two of Mr. Atkins' short-short poems and perform them. I have 'never' spent so much time memorizing in 'total' about 20 short lines. It was one of the rare occasions that I've been nervous prior to performing, and the 'first' time I've stepped up with paper in-hand for something I'd committed to memory. Like the title of this piece, taken from one of the two Atkins' poems I shared that day, I felt as if I was in a backyard back home reaching about for Mr. Atkins' words, praying I'd do them justice.

Tree Company

Yesterday my neighbor
pointed to the tree I see
from office window
one that frames road not taken
and told me 'It's dying.'
Me only giving attention
to supple branches
that wave each morning
green each Spring,
me missing the dead
brown reaching like Lurch
between the leaves, whispering
death, something I couldn't hear
till she brought it to my attention.

Tree Eulogy
7-17-15

I missed your birth
but story started by your mama goes
you made air so pure pollution
had to be added
so people could breathe
you grew tall and strong
a silent protest against
dogs who pissed on you
pet owners who let them
while resting under
shade you provided
free of charge.

Like most loved ones
I didn't realize
how much I cared
until it was too late

a neighbor's random comment
about an illness that should have been
obvious as my nose
slowly slowly
taking you down
one limb at a time
death slow as seasons passing
leaves fall and don't get up
and all that's left is time
a truck marked 'tree service'
and the sound of you cut up
like a dead body by a serial killer
shredded in a machine
that turns you into sawdust.

Tree Totem

What's left
sacred as breeze
stands on corner
its growl low
its roots paws
stamping ground
it roars
against die
spirit plants seeds
in me suddenly thirsty
for water
sun
new leaves.

Food fight
Wonder what?
was in #&!=<>
that house
13 yr old boy
left with his 16

& 6 yr. old brothers
they watch each other
mother works
mealtime
cupboards must have been
Hubbard's
food we eat to live
more important
a fight
for bites
not enough food
but a gun
13 yr old boy
could use
did use
ended the argument
gave himself the last
bullet—
word.

ZENA ZIPPORAH

On Russell Atkins

What I remember is the impish humor when he read his poems. But reading his poems for yourself is another matter. The staccato use of language sets him apart from the usual. His facility is that of a musician with words. Sound and meaning coagulate into a new form of expression. Bravo!

Living on the Line

is not always easy
your teeth chatter in Shaker Heights
as your toes are wiggling in Cleveland Heights
then you lose control and start babbling
about the dolls you once knew
about the statues you saw in Afghanistan
about how high the clouds are holding up
the maple trees and the sighs that slip out
between hairs, between the ointment you touched
and the sleep you lost.

Living on the line makes the earth a tower
when the church chimes do not work
hours are lost, motorcycles come racing up your fingers
and you lose control and start babbling
about the color blue and how it used to be
greener and how painful it is to
take in the blankets
and the memories of trips
to hemisphere where the light was clearer
and the food cleaner and pure orange.

You race over the line and stare him straight
in the eyes and start to gag
and know for once this is your only city
that you are unknown everywhere and will
be buried halfway to where sky meets clouds
and butterflies will pronounce you home.
Strange and lonely men are coming
The souls of the dead are coming.
Future lovers are coming.
The children of my children are coming.
The sun, moon, and stars are coming.
The minutes, seconds, and hours
of all future time are coming.

Coming

The illegal aliens are coming.
The iguana men are coming.
The melting of ice is coming.
Little blue men from outer space are coming.
The Russians are coming.
The lights of marauders are coming.
Jihadists with bombs sewn
in their underpants are coming.

The Poem

I am trying to write a poem
that you are not able to read
one that you must inhale
feeling it enter the pores
of your skin making a sound
only beetles can hear
a dance as delicate as
an ant walking across the room
that only the sound artist hears
a poem with colors imbedded in the words
the colors of the rainbow on Saturn's moon
loony and slippery as a ghost of a child
glimpsed in a mirror just before dawn
words in a language never heard
that disappears and takes with it
all memory like the life before death

Names

The artist kept a cage inside her.
Inside the cage were blue butterflies
that glowed in the night.
She called them by various names.
One was named after a plant in her garden,
a hearty kale that persisted in a pot.
One was named after a vowel
in a secret language
that she had created during
a long winter night.
One was named after her left eye
that always saw the sun
even on cloudy days
even when her lake froze over
and sent the geese squawking.
One was called house in honor
Of its rooms one after another
filled with things she had built
trying to set everything free
before it grew stiff with age
before it turned into the dust of forgetting.
And one was named after a solitary groan
of a wild animal dreaming of its own death.

POET BIOS

Russell Atkins

Russell Atkins is a major American avant garde poet of the second half of the twentieth century. He is also distinguished as a composer, editor (almost forty years with the important little magazine Free Lance), playwright, and musical theorist ("A Psychovisual Perspective for 'Musical' Composition"). His poetry has appeared in a number of chapbooks and has been gathered in his book *Here in The* (Cleveland: Cleveland State University Poetry Center, 1976) and in *Russell Atkins: On the Life & Work of an American Master, Kevin Prufer & Michael Dumanis*, eds. (Warrensburg, MO & Rock Hill, SC: Pleiades Press, 2013). Most of his poetry can also be found at the website of avant garde poetry, <eclipsearchive.org>, curated by Craig Dworkin. After more than eighty years in the city of Cleveland, Russell Atkins now lives in the nearby town of Oakwood.

In The Company of Russell Atkins:

Master Poet **Hzal Anubewei** is his name of enlightenment. He is a published poet, author, and playwright. He has appeared on radio and TV and was a writer in residence at Albany State in Albany, Georgia. He recently published a collection of short stories *A Scheme in Every Scene*.

Yaseen AsSami, born in Knoxville, Tennessee, attended school in a one-room school house through eighth grade and started writing in ninth grade, inspired by his English teacher, Mrs. Delainy. Arriving in Cleveland in 1966, he participated with Russell Atkins and Norman Jordan in the Muntu workshop. Recently, he has participated in the Cuyahoga County Public Library workshop and published poems in their yearly online anthology.

George Bilgere's poetry is well known to National Public Radio listeners through his many appearances on Garrison Keillor's

The Writer's Almanac and *A Prairie Home Companion*. Keillor has said, "No other American poet blends so skillfully the humorous with the sentimental." Bilgere's honors include grants and awards from the Cleveland Arts Prize, the Pushcart Foundation, the National Endowment for the Arts, the Ohio Arts Council, the Fulbright Foundation, and the May Swenson Poetry Award. Former U.S. Poet Laureate Billy Collins has called Bilgere's work "A welcome breath of fresh air in the house of American poetry." He teaches literature at John Carroll University in Cleveland.

John Donoghue's poetry has been anthologized in *The Book of Irish American Poetry* and has appeared in literary journals such as *Agni, Alaska Quarterly Review, Prairie Schooner,* and *The Virginia Quarterly Review* as well as in medical journals such as *The Lancet*. He is the author of the poetry collections *Precipice* and *A Small Asymmetry*.

Michael Dumanis is the author of *My Soviet Union*, winner of the Juniper Prize for Poetry. He coedited *Legitimate Dangers: American Poets of the New Century*, and, with Kevin Prufer, *Russell Atkins: On the Life & Work of An American Master*. Formerly Director of the Cleveland State University Poetry Center, he is now a professor at Bennington College and lives in New York.

A native Clevelander, **Leatrice Joy W. Emeruwa** is Professor Emerita at Cuyahoga Community College. She has published in several anthologies, including *Voices of Cleveland*, and is the author of two books, *Black Girl, Black Girl* and *Ev'ry shut eye ain't sleep, ev'ry goodbye ain't gon'!* As the Preacher-Poet, she sermonizes on Sunday broadcasts on WHKW, 1220 AM.

Christopher Franke, born on Christmas in 1941, started calling himself a "poet" in 1969. His chapbooks include *Title* (CSU Poetry Center 1975), *S.* (deciduous, 1977), *frankeana/miscellangy* (deciduous/wordedprint 1996), *Parens Thesis* (Burning Press 1997), select routines (P2B), *As the Caffeine Kicks In* (NightBallet Press 2013), and *Articals: a portfolio in progress for 3 ring notebook of 8 ½ x 11 poem-collage leaves* (deciduous).

John Gabel is a graduate of the Merchant Marine Academy and the University of Michigan in mathematics. He worked for four decades as an actuary. In mid-life he turned from numbers to words and began to study and write poetry through classes and workshops taught by Leonard Trawick and Alberta Turner at Cleveland State. He writes, "The half century I have spent listening to and writing poetry was perhaps the most rewarding of my 92 years on the planet."

Norman Jordan's poetry has been anthologized in 42 books, including *Black Fire* and *Make A Joyful Sound: Poems for Children by African American Poets* and in journals such as *Freelance*, *Vibration*, and *Confrontation*. His plays have been produced at Karamu House, among other venues. Along with Russell Atkins, Jordan was included by Langston Hughes in the classic, The Poetry of the Negro 1946-1970.

Diane Kendig --poet, writer, translator and teacher for over 40 years— has authored four poetry collections, most recently *Prison Terms*. A recipient of two Ohio Arts Council Poetry Fellowships, she has poems recently in *J Journal*, *Wordgathering*, and *Ekphrasis*, among others. She blogs on a variety of topics at Home Again.

Dawn Lundy Martin is author of *A Gathering of Matter/A Matter of Gathering*, *DISCIPLINE*, and *Life in a Box is a Pretty Life* (Nightboat 2015). Martin is co-founder of the Black Took Collective, an experimental performance art/poetry group, and Associate Professor of English at the University of Pittsburgh.

Robert E. McDonough has published two books of poems, *No Other World* and *Greatest Hits*, as well as numerous poems in little magazines and anthologies. After more than forty years of teaching English at Cuyahoga Community College in Cleveland, OH, he has retired to the Finger Lakes.

Ray McNiece is the author of eight books of poems and monologues. In a review of his second theatre work, *Us? Talking Across America*, the Star-Phoenix said, "His thoughtful writing combines with perfectly timed delivery to create a powerful wordscape that owes as much to jazz as drama."

Printmaker as well as poet, **Joan Nicholl** has published poems in anthologies such as *Voices of Cleveland* and journals such as *Whiskey Island*. She was an active member of the poetry scene in Cleveland for decades and continues her printmaking these days at the Cleveland Institute of Art.

Mwatabu S. Okantah, Associate Professor and Poet in Residence in the Kent State University Department of Pan-African Studies, has authored a spoken word CD and five books of poetry, most recently *Muntu Kuntu Energy: New and Selected Poetry* (2013). He lives in Akron, Ohio with his wife, Aminah, and their five children.

Nathan T. Oliver hails from Pittsburgh, Pennsylvania and was an early member of the Black Horizon Theater that spawned the "Center Avenue Street Poets" in the late sixties. He is the founder of the Charles Waddell Chesnutt Literary Society, which honors another important literary figure from Cleveland, Ohio.

Caryl Pagel is the author of two collections of poetry: *Twice Told* (H_NGM_N Books, 2014) and *Experiments I Should Like Tried at My Own Death* (Factory Hollow Press, 2012). She is an Assistant Professor of English at Cleveland State University and the Director of the Cleveland State University Poetry Center.

Kevin Prufer is the author of several poetry collections, most recently *National Anthem, In a Beautiful Country*, and Churches, named one of the New York Times' "Ten Favorite Poetry Books of 2014." He lives in Texas, where he is Professor of English in the Creative Writing Program at the University of Houston and co-curator of the Unsung Masters Series.

A native of Calcutta, **P.K. Saha** taught linguistics at Case Western Reserve University, served as Language & Etymology consultant for Webster's New World Dictionary, and has worked as a forensic linguist. He has published several hundred poems, stories, articles, reviews and books in Australia, England, India, Pakistan, and the USA.

M.A. Shaheed began writing in the seventh grade and first published in White motors newspaper under the name of Clyde Shy. He became a professional musician and continued to write but it wasn't on the front burner as he began to work on his spiritual development. He stopped writing for three decades but in recent years has published four books and been in five anthologies.

John Stickney is a poet/writer who lives and works in Cleveland, Ohio. In the 1980's and 1990's he was an active participant in the CSU and PLGC/PWLGC workshops. It was through these organizations and their community outreach activities that he got to know and appreciate Cleveland legend poet Russell Atkins.

Kent Taylor started writing poetry his freshman year at Ohio Wesleyan University. After quitting medical school at Ohio State University, he returned to Cleveland and joined its 1960s underground poetry scene. His first six books were published by d. a. levy. Taylor moved to San Francisco in 1970. His publications include 20 books and hundreds of appearances in anthologies and periodicals.

Leonard Trawick is a Professor Emeritus of English Literature at Cleveland State University. For a number of years he was chief editor of the CSU Poetry Center's series of poetry books, including Russell Atkins's collection *Here in The*.

Lewis Turco founded the Fenn College Poetry Center of Cleveland in 1962, six years before he published *the poet's Bible*, *The Book of Forms: A Handbook of Poetics*, now in its fourth edition. The author of more than fifty chapbooks, monographs and books, Turco's latest opus is *The Hero Enkidu, An Epic* (2015).

RA Washington's 25 books include *The Paris Notebooks* (Night-Ballet 2015) and the novel *CITI* (Red Giant Books, 2015). In 2014, Washington was awarded a Creative Workforce Fellowship from Cuyahoga Arts and Culture, and given a retrospective of his multi-media projects, music and writing in Montreal. He co-founded Guide To Kulchur, a bookstore, publishing imprint and show space in Cleveland's Historic Detroit Shoreway Neighborhood.

Mary E. Weems is a poet, playwright, author, and scholar. She is author and/or editor of thirteen books, most recently *Blackeyed: Plays and Monologues* and *For(e)closure* a finalist for an Ohioana Book Award. Weems is a lifelong Clevelander and lover of words. She won the 2015 Cleveland Arts Prize for Literature.

Zena Zipporah's main avocation has been visual art containing and concerning language, but she has written poetry since her college work at SUNY-Buffalo (BA) and Case Western Reserve University (MA). She has had many exhibitions, publications, and awards. In 2013, she received one of Cleveland's Community Partnership for Arts and Culture Awards.

Credits

Hzal Anubewei. "Eyes," "Father," and "Pouring Shade," © 2015 by Hzal Anubewei. Used by permission of the author.

Russell Atkins. "Homeless," "Over His Dead Body," and "Threnodic Phantasies for Example" first published in *The Chestnutt Record* © 1988 by Russell Atkins. Reprinted by permission of the author. "DAWN Rest Home," © 2015 by Russell Atkins. Used by permission of the author.

John Donoghue. "In the design review meeting He said" first published in *A Small Asymmetry*, © 2005 by John Donoghue. Reprinted by permission of the author. "Solstice" first published in *A Small Asymmetry*, © 2005 by John Donoghue. Reprinted by permission of the author. "Revision" first published in *The Virginia Quarterly Review*, © 1998 John Donoghue. Reprinted by permission of the author.

Michael Dumanis. "Squalor" first published in *Ploughshares*, © 2011 by Michael Dumanis. Reprinted by permission of the author. "Clouds" first published *The Book of Scented Things: 100 Contemporary Poems about Perfume*, © 2014 by Michael Dumanis. Reprinted by permission of the author. "The Forecast" first published in *The Academy of American Poets Poem-a-Day Project*, © 2011 by Michael Dumanis. Reprinted by permission of the author.

Leatrice J. W. Emeruwa. "'bout Mahalia" © 2000 by Leatrice W. Emeruwa. Used by permission of the author. "To My Dark Lover" first published in *Black Girl, Black Girl*, ©1972 by Leatrice W. Emeruwa. Reprinted by permission of the author. "Do The Old Still Love?" © 1995 by Leatrice W. Emeruwa. Used by permission of the author.

Robert Fleming. "For Russell, the Alchemist" © 2015 by Robert Fleming. Used by permission of the author. "Cullud Maumau" first published in *Melons*, © 1972 by Robert Fleming. Reprinted by permission of the author. "666" first published in *Melons*, © 1972 by Robert Fleming. Reprinted by permission of the author.

Franke, Chris. "O, Let'er Press," "Going to the Well, but Hell," and "BAR" ©2016 by Chris Franke. Used by permission of the author.

John Gabel. "Live Oak" first published in *John Gabel Greatest Hits*, © 2002 by John Gabel. Reprinted by permission of the author. "The S.S. Meteor" and "there is something" first published in *Beach Glass*, Poems by John Gabel, © 1979 by John Gabel. Reprinted by permission of the author.

Norman Jordan. "One Eyed Critics" first published in *Destination Ashes*, © 1970 by Norman Jordan. Reprinted by permission of the author. "I Was Cool" first published in *Where Do People In Dreams Come From?* © 2004 by Norman Jordan. Reprinted by permission of the author. "For My Sons: Neogriots" first published in *Where Do People In Dreams Come From?* © 2006 by Norman Jordan. Reprinted by permission of the author.

Diane Kendig. "Visiting Russell Atkins with Alarm" © 2015 by Diane Kendig. Used by permission of the author. "Mushfake" first published in *J Journal: New Writing on Justice*, © 2009 by Diane Kendig. Reprinted by permission of the author. "The Forest Animals' Diversions" first published in *The Seventh Quarry: Swansea Poetry Magazine* © 2010 by Diane Kendig. Reprinted by permission of the author. "A Double Abecedarian for NaPoWrMo" first published in *Common Threads*, © 2014 by Diane Kendig. Reprinted by permission of the author.

Dawn Lundy Martin. From Good Stock first appeared in *Good Stock on the Dimension Floor (a film by Howdoyousayyaminafrican?, a global artists collective)* ©2014 by Dawn Lundy Martin. Reprinted by permission of the author.

McDonough, Robert E. "A Favor for Orpheus," "A Good Drinker," "2014," and "High Summer" ©2016 by Robert E. McDonough. Used by permission of the author.

Ray McNiece. "Boneyard," "Drips," and "Skull Relief" ©2015 by Ray McNiece. Used by permission of the author.

Praise for Doc Smo

"At a time when the internet contains a diverse array of opinions on parenting, Dr. Smolen's book provides something important– **a voice of reason that parents can use for guidance.**"

–Jon Abramson, M.D.
Former Chairperson, World Health Organization
Strategic Advisory Group of Experts on Immunization
Former Chair of the Department of Pediatrics
Wake Forest School of Medicine

"**Practical, relevant help for today's parents.**"

–John Rosemond, family psychologist,
author of *The Well-Behaved Child*

"**Doc Smo provides many nuggets of wisdom,** such as praise the effort, not the child. And his stories about children, as told through the eyes of an experienced pediatrician, are a bonus."

–Landis Wade, award-winning author of *The Christmas Redemption,*
Charlotte Readers Podcast

"This helpful and warm-hearted book reinforces **a crucial lesson for parents: you can make a difference.**"

–Roy Benaroch, M.D. *The Pediatric Insider*

"Dr. Paul Smolen has helped parents optimize their children's diet, health, character, and balance. **Now his insights are available to everyone.**"

–The Charlotte Observer

Great Kids
Don't Just Happen

5 Essentials for Raising Successful Children

Great Kids
Don't Just Happen

5 Essentials for Raising Successful Children

Paul Smolen, M.D.

Edited by Annie Beth Donahue

Torchflame Books

Durham, NC

Published 2019, by Torchflame Books
www.lightmessages.com
Durham, NC 27713 USA
SAN: 920-9298

Paperback ISBN: 978-1-61153-299-9
E-book ISBN: 978-1-61153-294-4
Library of Congress Control Number: 2019913157

For the past 37 years, it has been my privilege to help children and families live healthier and happier lives. I wrote this book to share what I have observed during my career, with the hope of making the next generation of children spectacularly successful.

This book is dedicated to all the children of this and future generations.

Contents

Acknowledgments

Anyone who has ever written a book knows that you don't go at this alone. It is not a solo sport. It is, rather, the culmination of many people's efforts and thoughts. I would like to thank those who helped give me the insight and energy to complete this book:

—Wendy Smolen, my wife who gives me inspiration and wisdom regularly.

—Sarah and Benjamin Smolen, my adult children, whose support and guidance has been invaluable to my completion of this book and creation of my blog/podcast.

—Annie Beth Donahue, my editor, who sharpens both my thinking and expression.

—Dr. Stephen DeCherney, for helping improve my book with his editorial commentary.

—Dr. Charlotte Rouchouze, a fellow blogger, who often challenges my thinking with her insights and wisdom.

—David Ross, my longtime friend, tennis adversary, and writing cheerleader.

—Drs. John Plonk, Stephen Valder, and Monica Miller, who provided their critiques and insights during the writing of this book.

—Seth Jaffe, Esquire, who steadfastly and wisely helps me navigate the creative, legal, and technical landscape in which we live.

—The thousands of parents and children whom I have met during my pediatric career. Many thanks for sharing your wisdom and insights with me.

—Wally, Betty, and Elizabeth Turnbull along with the staff at Light Messages Publishing, for helping my manuscript reach publication with such style.

Introduction

You may be asking yourself, "Are there essential things parents need to provide for their children in order for them to thrive and become Great Kids? And if there is such a magic formula, how would a pediatrician—an expert trained in childhood diseases—know what constitutes optimal parenting? Did he learn these things in anatomy or biochemistry class?"

Of course not. So what qualifies me to make such important pronouncements? How in the world would I know what constitutes good versus suboptimal parenting? For that matter, how can anyone be so presumptuous as to claim to know such things?

It is true; I have no degree in counseling. I have done no formal study of human psychology other than my observations during my thirty-seven years of clinical practice of pediatrics.

But think about it. Thirty-seven years of day-to-day conversations and observations of the intimate workings of families. That is a powerful database.

This gives pediatricians (like myself) a unique look at children and families over a very extended period of time. We are able to see firsthand how different families mold and shape their children from newborn, all the way to adulthood.

Pediatricians See the End Game

Pediatricians see how different family scenarios function day-to-day and how parents and children communicate with one another. And pediatricians who are lucky enough to practice for a very long time in the same location, with the same families, are privileged to see what happens to many of these children when they become grown. *We get to see the end game.*

I have a front row seat to observe parents' struggle with the very considerable demands that newborns present. I watch as these new families develop the parent-child bond. I get to see them struggle with enforcing limits with their toddlers. I'm right there to support families and children as they enter the competitive academic world. I watch and advise parents as they mold their child's character, teach them manners, enjoy the child's accomplishments and react to their disappointments. I watch it all and observe.

Fortunately, many, if not most, of the children who graduate from my care become incredible adults—confident, energetic, humble, intelligent young adults—ready to take on the world. But some are less well-equipped, and I believe there are reasons for this.

Childhood is all about growth, change, and development. That's where parents come in. I believe that parents need to understand that they must provide fundamental, essential ingredients for their children to optimize their growth and development. **Parents are responsible for creating the environment that shapes their children's personalities.**

Yes, genetics, life circumstances, and temperament factor into the formula. But I believe that the effect of parenting is much stronger. Thirty-seven years of observing family interactions has convinced me that parenting matters. Parents who fail to provide any of the five parenting essentials we are about to discuss in this book are in danger of impeding their children's healthy psychological development, physical well-being, and adult happiness.

This book contains current research and leading thought about parenting, along with real-life observations from my career. Reading it can help you effectively and successfully rear your own families. My hope is that not only will parents with young children read this book but also other adults—grandparents, educators, pediatricians, and all those who care for children.

Layout of the Book

Now for the layout of the book. The five main chapters of my book have a similar structure. Each chapter identifies a core characteristic that families provide for their children to improve their chances of having optimal growth and development.

I begin each of these five chapters with a description of the type of families I have cared for who illustrate some aspect of this core characteristic. While none of my fictional families exist in reality, they are based on aggregates of numerous families I have known. Think of them as composites of real families. None of these families actually exist and any overlap with real persons, either in name or in description, is totally by coincidence.

Next comes a discussion of relevant current research that amplifies the debate and provides some context for the discussion—what I call "Science Drive."

Finally, each chapter ends with a chapter summary and an analysis of why some parents have trouble providing the core characteristic discussed in that chapter.

But before we get into the main chapters, I begin the book with a chapter about the changing structure of the American family that—in some ways—may make parenting more difficult. Now more than ever, it is critical that all parents, regardless of family structure, understand what their children need to become Great Kids.

Society is evolving and changing, but children still need what they need—the same things that they have always needed. *That has not changed, and I suspect never will.* It is your and my responsibility to do our best to provide for all their needs. The next generation is depending on our guidance. **We can't let them down.**

1

Raising Great Kids in Today's America

"Making the babies was the easy part of parenting!"

—Doc Smo *Pearl*
Portable Practical Pediatrics Podcast
November 26, 2013

The world is changing but the fundamentals of good parenting have not.

The pace of change in the modern world has accelerated to an unprecedented speed. And these changes have occurred in almost all aspects of our lives—including raising children. If you are a parent today, I'm sure you can feel it. Consider these facts: technology has compressed the speed of our travel, accelerated our ability to communicate with one another, turbocharged the dissemination of information, and allowed the average adult and child to use technologies that are truly futuristic.

Experts call this rate of change "exponential," meaning ever faster and more intense. These advances strengthen our connection with the rest of the world. But technology seems to be devaluing the influence of a child's family by *reducing* the impact of the immediate family while *increasing* a child's exposure to the outside influence of movies, social media, and peers.

I think you have to admit that the internet, smartphones, and social media have fundamentally changed the lives of children. Now add to these technological changes the fact that the structure and composition of families are also undergoing a metamorphosis.

You can see that today's parents have to adapt to these changes if they are to raise a Great Kid. (A term I define in a few pages.)

In so many ways, this era of cultural and technological flux has made the already challenging job of raising children even more difficult. But it's not *impossible* to grow Great Kids. If today's parents have an understanding of the *core things that their children need,* and they are able to consistently deliver those things for them, the distractions of intrusive technologies and alternative family structures will be simply that—just distractions.

I believe the fundamental principles of good parenting have not changed even though the world clearly has. Following these principles will give your children such a strong foundation that they will be able to handle whatever life has in store for them. Good parenting trumps our exponentially changing world. Consider the story of April.

The Story of April:

April was sixteen years old the day I saw her in my office for a sick visit, accompanied by her mother. Her complaint was abdominal pain and urinary frequency. As I explored her history by asking April questions away from her mother, I discovered that she had missed her last period, was sexually active, and worried she could be pregnant.

I could sense her anxiety that she might be pregnant as soon as we touched on the subject. Sure enough, her examination, blood count, and urine were normal, but her pregnancy test was unequivocally positive. April's only health issue that day was that she was pregnant. A tragedy and crisis for many teens.

Most sixteen-year-olds have very few resources to deal with such a serious situation: no high school diploma, no husband, and no independence from their families. Adding to April's problems was the fact that I was about to deliver this life-changing news with her mother very much involved in her visit to my office. Awkward is an extreme understatement to describe April's situation.

I have to be honest, I dreaded having to go back in that room and break the news to April. But I needed to help her through this difficult situation. Before I returned to her exam room, I gathered a few phone numbers of community resources that she might find helpful in dealing with what I expected would be an unwanted pregnancy.

I entered the room, ready to witness a flood of emotion from both April and her mother. However, rather than hysteria and anger, I witnessed both April and her mother process what I was telling them and then rapidly gather their composure. They weren't happy with this event, but they weren't devastated either.

Since this was a first-trimester pregnancy, we talked over options. I offered April numbers of places where she could get abortion services. "No," she said, "I'm not going that way. Abortion is off the table." That is something she and her mother agreed on. "Ok," I said, "Let's think about the situation and talk again in a week."

A week went by, and sure enough, April and her mother returned to my office for another chat. April and her mother both still felt that the pregnancy should go on. But so would April's plans for her life. No shotgun weddings. No forced love affairs. April's high school studies would continue, even if that meant she had to attend a special school for pregnant teens. When her baby was old enough for daycare, April intended to return to school and finish her education. And indeed, she lived up to that promise.

After her baby son was born, I was lucky enough to become his pediatrician. April always brought her son for his appointments and was very engaged with his health care, raising very relevant questions and concerns. April turned out to be a great mom. Being a single parent with a limited education didn't paralyze her. She had no difficulty getting her son to adjust to the family's schedules, transitioning him to solid foods, or creating a safe environment for him. April wasn't shy about depending heavily on her mother for help, but I saw her willingness to ask for help as a strong positive. Her mother was one of April's greatest strengths.

April did finish high school, and after a year off, started community college to study nursing. The father of her baby gradually lost interest and faded out of their lives, but April and her extended family were able to provide her son with a warm, loving household in which to grow up. Material things were sparse; love was abundant. Over the years, I lost touch with April and her son, but at last sight, both April and her son were thriving.

I was always amazed at April's determination to make the most of her situation from the moment I gave her the news of her unwanted pregnancy. I don't believe that April secretly wanted this pregnancy. No, I think she was just able to accept responsibility for her actions and make the best of the situation in which she found herself.

A Pediatrician's Perspective of April and Her Family

From my vantage point, April and her family are amazing people. I have confidence that April, along with her family, will continue to provide her son with many of the ingredients I see in healthy families—those families that produce Great Kids. After spending a few years watching April, it was apparent to me that April's mother had been able to raise a very resilient daughter. And she was well on her way to passing that resiliency onto her son. From a pediatrician's perspective, I must say it was a very positive experience. One that gave me great hope for the future.

Take a minute to consider what April was able to accomplish. She and her family took a situation that many would have considered a tragedy, and they morphed their unexpected circumstance into a blessing. How did they do this? By providing many of the core characteristics I see in families who produce Great Kids.

April's family was raising their child in a household possessing a healthy emotional environment (Chapter 4), committing a lot of the family's energy to their child's wellbeing (Chapter 5), and providing a stable environment in which their child can grow (Chapter 6).

April's story is a perfect example of how parenting shapes children. As my title points out, *Great Kids Don't Just Happen*. No, there are forces at play that every family needs to keep in mind as their children grow and mature. The ingredients that April and her family leveraged for her son are the secret sauce that allows them and other families to thrive and produce Great Kids.

"A Detour Down Science Drive"—How the Changing American Family is Affecting Children

Let's start our discussion about raising great kids by taking a closer look at the incubator for the growth of children—their families. For better or worse, the two-parent family with parents bound by legal marriage is becoming rarer. More children are being raised in alternative families and by parents who have fewer financial and emotional supports than previous generations enjoyed.

There is no doubt that the variety of family structures has increased in recent years. Unfortunately, the stability of many families has diminished during the same period of time. The era of an intergenerational traditional family is disappearing in contemporary America and is being replaced by alternative families: single-parent households, grandparent-headed households, blended families, unmarried cohabiting couples, families headed by same-sex couples, and transgender men giving birth.

The composition of the "family" is broader in twenty-first century America than it was in previous generations. The fundamental unit that has raised children in the past is changing fast. You will find much more discussion about the influence of a child's family on their well-being in subsequent chapters.

Add to the shift in family structure the fact that the number of external influences has also been growing steadily. The power of the images and messaging from *screens* (TVs, smartphones, tablets, or computers) has diminished the influence a *family* has on the thoughts and behaviors of their children. Digital communications have also heightened peer influence, all while exposing children to elements of society that parents may find less than optimal.

Studies confirm the drastic change to the family unit in the U.S. in the past half-century. The Pew Research group has analyzed the structure of the American family over the past fifty-three years. The trends they discovered are dramatic. For instance, in 1960, 73% of children were born into families with first-time married parents in the United States. By 1980 the rate had fallen to 61%, and in 2013 the percentage had dropped to 46%.[1] In other words, in America today, **the majority of children are being raised in families without first-time married two-parent households.**

Family Composition 2013 America

	Households Headed by 1st Marriage-Two parents	Single Parent Households	Blended Households	Non Parent Households
1960	73%	9%	14%	4%
1980	61%	19%	16%	4%
2013	46%	34%	15%	5%

Pew Family Research 2013[1]

Much of the fall in the number of households headed by two parents is due to the dramatic rise in the number of children who are living with only one biological parent. This is for many reasons including divorce, parental abandonment, or the increasingly common out-of-wedlock birth that is sometimes being made by choice.[2] In this case, Pew Research found that the percentage of children who lived with only one parent in the U.S. has risen steadily in the past fifty-three years: 1960=9%, 1980=19%, and 2013 reaching 34%.[1]

Given all of this turmoil in the American family, it is not surprising that families are becoming more isolated

Given all of this turmoil in the American family, it is not surprising that families are becoming more isolated. Sociologists McPhearson, Lovin, and Brashears discovered a dramatic rise in social isolation of adults when they analyzed the data from the General Social Survey between the years 1985 and 2004.[3]

In this survey, adults were asked how many "confidants,"— kin or non-kin—they could discuss important life issues with. Presumably, the larger the number of "confidants" a parent had, the less socially isolated they were at the time.

In 2004, the respondents had 33% fewer people they could rely on to help make life decisions or sort through life's problems than they did in 1985. The researchers felt that this change indicated a significant rise in social isolation of parents in 2004 relative to 1985.

Not only was the average number of confidants dropping during these decades, but when asked how many trusted confidants they had, the most frequent answer by the 2004 respondents *was zero!* You don't get any more socially isolated than that.

Stated another way, **parents who had zero people to turn to to help make life decisions for their family comprised the largest group of parents.** A hard place to find oneself, especially as a parent of young children.

Finally, as if all these negative trends weren't stressful enough for families in the U.S., according to the nonprofit advocacy group Child Trends, the rate of extreme childhood poverty (defined as living at 50% of the poverty level of family income) among American children has doubled between 1973 and 2014. This number rose from 5% to 9.5%.[4] Less stable family structure among more socially isolated parents who are increasingly living in poverty paints a grim trend for many of today's children.

Making Sense of the Data: Why is all this data important to today's parents?

It appears that the changing American family is not doing good things for many American children. As you just learned, more of today's children are being born into families under stress. These children are being raised by a single parent who is socially isolated and living in extreme poverty. Their stars seem to be aligned in a negative fashion. American culture is moving into previously unknown territory with regards to family structure and its impact on the well-being of children.

As a pediatrician involved in the day-to-day lives of children, I witnessed this rapid change during my career. *But despite the negative shift that is occurring, families are still succeeding in raising Great Kids.* I see them do it all the time—no matter how big the obstacles seem. Just like April, when families get the basics right, Great Kids just happen. Provide what children really need, and the rest will fall into place. As you will see in forthcoming chapters, these core characteristics are:

1. A parent or parents who know how to effectively use praise with their children.

2. Parents who know how to and are willing to set age appropriate limits for their children.

3. A family with a healthy emotional climate.

4. Parents with a strong emotional investment in their children's success.

5. A household that maximizes stability.

These are things that I feel—and you are about to see why—are the essential tools of successful parents. They are the characteristics I see in the healthiest families that I care for and the ones most likely to raise a Great Kid.

If you were able to ask your great-great-grandmother what makes Great Kids and successful parenting, she would likely point out these same family traits as essential to raising emotionally healthy children. She understood how paramount families are to the children that they parent. Great-great-grandmother also understood that, *regardless of the obstacles,* she needed to provide these traits for the children she was raising.

Defining Parenting Success

The American Academy of Pediatrics (AAP) recognizes the significant influence families have on the ultimate outcomes for the children that they raise. The AAP describes a child's family as the greenhouse for the growth of their children. "Children's social, emotional, and physical health; their developmental trajectory; and the neurocircuits that are being created and reinforced in their developing brains are all directly influenced by their relationships during early childhood."[5]

> *The influence of a child's parents and family is the most important factor in their ultimate success in life.*

The influence of a child's parents and family is the most important factor in their ultimate success in life. You will see this play out in the following chapters. I show how experiences, lessons learned, and love received serve to build the foundation of a child's personality, resilience, and ultimate happiness and achievement.

But first, our discussion of parenting success needs to start with the definition of success. What do I mean when I speak of raising a Great Kid or Great Young Adult—the product of parenting success stories? I am sure there are many definitions. And these definitions are bound by cultural norms and practices. However, for the purposes of this book I intend to use my personal definition.

My Definition of a Great Kid/Young Adult

For me, parents and families have achieved success in raising Great Kids when their children can do the following things by the time they reach young adulthood:

1. Be self-sufficient.

2. Maintain stable employment.

3. Create and maintain long-term friendships and family relationships.

4. Live without substance abuse dependency.

5. Be generally happy and emotionally stable.

6. Abide by the laws of society.

Note that my definition of a successful young adult demands that, as a child, they not only *mastered a set of skills* (self-sufficiency) and *have a fairly high level of self-control* (abide by laws, do not have problems with substance abuse, and maintain stable employment), but also that they *have a sensitivity to the significant people in their lives* (have stable long-term relationships).

How do parents instill all of this in their children? What are those parenting skills that create the successful child, the Great Kid and young adult? That's what I will help you discover in the next five chapters.

Can different family configurations produce successful children?

Is there a certain family structure that guarantees good outcomes for the children that they produce? I think it is fair to say there is not. It is the *quality of the parenting and family environment that determines outcome* rather than the family structure per se.

Successful children can come from many different backgrounds, as you will soon see. But there are *common features* among the families that consistently produce Great Kids. I have witnessed this firsthand during my pediatric career.

Now You Know

- The contemporary American family is changing rapidly.
- The family and parenting environment that produces Great Kids is the same as it always has been.
- The increasing challenges of family isolation, single-parent households, and poverty make producing Great Kids more challenging—but definitely achievable.
- Children who become successful adults have a defined set of attitudes and skills that they were taught and mastered during their childhoods.
- Experienced pediatricians have insight into how families create Great Kids.

What Can You Do?

1. Learn the essential ingredients that healthy families provide for their children.
2. Understand how important parenting is to a child's future.
3. Always strive to do your best to create an emotionally healthy environment for your children.

2

A Parent's Use of Praise

*"It's a terrible mistake for parents
to underestimate their influence
on their kids."*

—Doc Smo *Pearl*
Portable Practical Pediatrics Podcast
September 12, 2016

The Story of Katherine:

Katherine was the first-born child to a middle-class family living in the suburbs. Both of her parents were college educated. Her mother was a teacher and her father an accountant. When Katherine arrived, her parents, like most, were ecstatic. Their camera didn't stop shooting photos of their newest family member. Anyone who spent even a modicum of time with Katherine's family realized that her parents adored her—especially her mother. Her mom just wouldn't stop talking about how beautiful and precocious Katherine was.

She was pretty easy as babies go—cute, playful, and happy most of the time. When Katherine got to school age, the adoration continued. I personally heard Katherine's mother say on many occasions, "Katherine, you are sooo beautiful." Or other things like, "Katherine, I have never met a child as smart as you are." "Katherine, you are amazing." "Katherine, you are such a great athlete." "Katherine, you are a superstar."

When adolescence came, the parental fan club didn't stop. You could tell, however, that Katherine was becoming uneasy with her parents and their worship of her achievements, beauty, and athletic prowess. By now Katherine knew that anything short of top performance would disappoint her parents. She also knew that her parents' praise, while flattering, was unrealistic. She was not Katherine the Magnificent. She was just Katherine. And she knew it.

To protect herself from failure, Katherine started avoiding any activity that involved competition. In fact, she would get quite upset when asked to participate in an athletic or academic challenge. She became withdrawn and moody. Her inner turmoil led to her having problems with both her peers and family. Her friends misperceived her insecurity as conceit and snobbery. Her family had trouble talking to her and emotionally connecting with her struggles. Katherine was becoming quite emotionally isolated.

Why was this happening to Katherine—someone who seemed to have all the support and love in the world? Here is my guess. It seemed as though all the praise she had gotten through her childhood, rather than making her confident and self-assured, had had the opposite effect. Katherine strongly feared failure and lacked confidence in herself. After college, she married her first serious boyfriend.

In her young adult years, Katherine was somewhat immature. She continued to party like a late teen, displaying heavy drinking tendencies and adolescent behavior. She ultimately chose a career that required very little responsibility.

To me, it seemed that she never really achieved the degree of success that her parents expected. Her parents' excessive praise through her formative years had made her risk-averse and very afraid of failure. I believe their inability to realistically assess their daughter's strengths and weaknesses also stifled her maturing process. At 22, I saw a young adult who was acting more like a 15-year-old.

A pediatrician's perspective of Katherine and her family

Katherine's story is an all-too-common example of parents who delay their child's healthy development by overindulging them with praise. These parents give their children an unrealistic, inflated view of their own talents, presumably to improve their self-esteem. All well-meaning but destructive none-the-less.

As you are about to see, heaping undeserved praise on a child impairs their ability to develop the needed skill of self-assessment. When a child's every action is praised and inflated, they are not able to develop an accurate vision of their strengths and weaknesses.

In this chapter we will explore these themes and help guide new parents toward a healthy balance in their use of praise, criticism, and natural consequences. Love, encouragement, and protection are natural emotions for parents to direct toward their children. This is healthy and normal. But as Katherine's story demonstrates, there is a line between the healthy and destructive use of these parental emotions.

I feel that Katherine's family crossed that line, making Katherine's childhood more difficult and ultimately impairing her ability to put all of her energy into positive growth.

What are the forces that move children to mature as they grow older?

Fortunately, most children grow up to become responsible, happy, productive adults. How does this happen? What forces forge their development into such great adults?

Ask most older parents and grandparents (those who have seen a generation or two come of age) and I bet you will hear them repeat many of the same themes:

- Children need to learn to *accept responsibility* for their actions.

- Children need to learn to *make good behavior choices* by experiencing failure and learning from the consequences of that failure.

- Children need to learn to *see the world from other people's point of view* and learn to *compromise and have empathy*.

- Children need to have the patience and motivation to *master life skills* in their move toward independence. Accepting failure is an important part of that process.

- Children need to *learn social skills* like sharing, respect for others, honesty, and self-sacrifice.

Think about this list of skills that foster maturity in children. Now ask yourself, "Can an overpraised child can master these skills?"

Common sense tells me that a child who is either overpraised or over criticized will have great difficulty achieving these goals.

When the parental message to the child is, "You are greatest, no matter what," a child has already received a parent's approval without even attempting whatever the task at hand may be. That task at hand might be academics, or soccer skills, or musical ability—but little effort is given. Success is assured because parental confirmation of excellence will always be there. *The praise comes no matter what.*

Alternately, in the case of consistently critical reviews and feedback by a parent, the child will also become less likely to try learning the new task at hand. They know all they'll receive is disapproval. Failure is imminent.

In both cases—excessive praise or criticism—the child becomes less likely to learn and grow from their experiences; emotional growth is thereby slowed. And without that growth in maturity, these children are destined to fall behind their peers in the journey to adulthood. Excessive praise or criticism interferes with the normal maturing process that is so vital to a growing child.

Here is another way to look at the same list, from the perspective of a child's development of behavioral self-control. Psychologist and physician, Dr. Leonard Sax, argues in his book, *The Collapse of Parenting*, that the essential personality feature of children who go on to become successful adults is *self-control*.[1]

Dr. Sax argues that children who exhibit the highest degree of self-control are those who are destined to have the most success in life. With this fact in mind, reread the list above. You will see that mastering each of these tasks leads to a high degree of self-control.

Accepting responsibility for one's actions, making good behavior choices, learning to understand the perspective of others, having the patience to master a myriad of life's practical and social skills all require practicing and increasing your level of self-control. In fact, I believe that what we call *maturation* is actually a reflection of growth in a child's mastery of *self-control*.

"A Detour Down Science Drive"—The ABCs of Operant Conditioning

One of the most important duties parents have is to mold their children's behavior so that it is constructive and socially acceptable. Somehow parents need to tame their child's innate narcissism and obsession with themselves and redirect their behavior to conform to social norms.

In other words, *parents are tasked with changing a child's thoughts and actions that are dominated by "Me" to an attitude of "Us."* But what tools do parents have at their disposal to achieve this goal? How do parents interact with their kids to move them away from being self-centered and develop an attitude of graciousness and cooperation toward others?

Some of the most obvious factors that shape a child's behavior are: things a child receives that motivate a particular behavior (such as the gift of a toy), a privilege (such as attending a movie or a special trip to the park), or something simple like the praise of his or her parents.

Behavioral psychologists call these types of rewards *positive reinforcers*. They are *positive* in that the reward the child receives is a pleasant thing. They are *reinforcing* in that they tend to motivate the child to repeat the behavior.

When a child's environment responds to a behavior in a negative way, we call it *punishment* or *negative reinforcers*. *Punishment* can also alter behavior, as we all know so well. Examples of *punishment* in a child's environment are: a spanking, loss of privileges, isolation, and of course, verbal disapproval of a child's actions. While all of these punishments are unpleasant for a child, they definitely shape future behavior.[2]

Another set of forces that mold a child's behavior are ones that are not imposed on the child, but instead, are *natural consequences* of the behavior. These are usually events that occur from some action or inaction on the part of the child. Examples of natural consequences are: failing a test due to lack of studying, losing a friend by making an insensitive remark to their buddy, or having no money because a child spent rather than saved some of their allowance.

In some respects, natural consequences are the strongest shapers of a child's behavior, and they don't even require parental action! Those readers who have listened to my podcast or read my blog are familiar with what I call "Doc Smo *Pearls*"—short thoughts meant to reinforce an important parenting message. So here is one Doc Smo pearl for you: "Children learn quickest when their actions (or inactions) have consequences."

One final tool parents use to create Great Kids

In addition to the previously mentioned psychological factors that affect a child's behaviors, another powerful determinant of how a child will behave is mimicry, or imitation of the behavior the child sees in others. "Who do children have to mimic," you ask? Their parents and siblings of course.

The most important behavior a child learns to mimic is that of their parents. Normal behavior for a young child is the behavior they witness around them. These interactions constitute the *entire reality* of their world. If it is common to see Dad hit Mom, or witness Mom throwing things at Dad, these behaviors become normal to the children of that household.

> *The most important behavior a child learns to mimic is that of their parents.*

Conversely, if a child sees parents who communicate well and have mutual respect, that becomes normal for them. Children are always watching how their parents behave (or don't behave) and internalize what they see as normal.

What's the saying? "Do as I say and not as I do." When parents model poor behavior or ideals for their children, trying to tell those same children to act ethically is bound to fail. We all know that this approach doesn't work to shape a child's behavior. Children mimic what they see and experience far more than they respond to verbal instructions.

Leading by providing a positive example sends a powerful signal to a child as to how they should behave—an example that is hard for them to ignore. (We will be exploring this theme in more depth in Chapter 6.)

Praise or criticism: Which works better?

We have all heard the expression, "Carrots work better than sticks when it comes to changing behavior." Is this really true? Well, maybe. Positive reinforcers (rewards and praise) strengthen a particular behavior that a parent wants to see from a child.

Punishment tends to weaken it and at the same time create hesitancy, anxiety, and aggression in a child's future behavior.[3]

So if punishment has negative effects on children's behavior, and rewards reinforce the desired behaviors, then parents should use as much reward as possible in order to get a child who exhibits the behaviors that the parent wants—right?

Well, no. It turns out that if the carrots are too easy to get, or come with little effort, a child's motivations and willingness to *even try* become weakened. This effect has been coined "The Inverse Power of Praise."[4]

Said another way, excessive praise can have the opposite effect on a child than the parents intend. It can weaken, rather than strengthen, the child's eagerness to try and succeed. I see this pretty commonly in children like Katherine, the vignette I presented at the beginning of this chapter.

What happens to children when their parents' view of them is not realistic?

Parents have a powerful influence on their children's ultimate personality and emotional health. Think about your friends with children who are optimistic about life, who are willing to work hard, who are altruistic and empathetic toward others. I'll bet more often than not, they have children who turn out with the same traits. Children get infused with their parents' emotional reactions during their childhoods. The lens that parents use to understand the world around them is passed down to their children.

A good example of this is religion. Religious beliefs (regardless of the particular religion) are a set of beliefs that give their followers a way to see the world. Don't believe that parents have such a strong effect on their children? Just consider the fact that most adult children follow the religious tradition in which they were raised, even if their commitment to that religion was not very strong during their childhoods. This is a perfect example of the intergenerational influence on a child's worldview- the lens a child ultimately uses to view the world and judge the actions of others.

But what happens if parents create a reality for their children that is not realistic or sustainable? This happens when children are raised by parents who assume their child will become a superstar professional athlete, a famous movie star, or (as the story of Katherine portrays) a perfect child and adult.

For 99.9% of children, none of these inflated achievements are realistic or will ever materialize. Giving a child the impression that they are far more talented, smart, and attractive than the other children around them—possessing talent that others can only envy—is not only unrealistic but harmful to their ultimate ability to evaluate their own talents compared to others.

These parents, while well-meaning, are giving their children a worldview that will not serve them well in the long run. Even though Katherine's parents interpreted every action she made as amazing, as she grew she began to understand that the rest of the world didn't see her the way her parents did. Katherine eventually realized that her parents had an unreasonable view. She could never live up to their expectations.

Eventually Katherine realized she couldn't perform at the level her parents' expectations demanded—so she simply stopped trying. She eventually came to the painful conclusion that, in the eyes of those outside her family, she was more ordinary than spectacular. This made her progressively more hesitant to attempt new challenges. Quite the opposite effect her family had intended! Katherine experienced the "Inverse Power of Praise."

"A Detour Down Science Drive"—The Effect of Praise on Children

In their book, *Nurture Shock*, Bronson and Merriman present an excellent discussion of praise research.[4] They refer to the negative effects of excessive praise as the "Inverse Power of Praise."

Bronson and Merriman describe in detail much of the research with regards to praising children, and they lay out its positive and negative effects. They primarily focus on the research of Carol Dweck, a psychology professor at Stanford University. Here is their description of Dr. Dweck's seminal research:

> "Dweck sent four female research assistants into New York fifth-grade classrooms. The researchers would take a single child out of the classroom for a nonverbal IQ test consisting of a series of puzzles— puzzles easy enough that all the children would do fairly well. Once the child finished the test, the researchers told each student his score, then gave him a single line of praise. Randomly divided into groups, some were praised for their intelligence. They were told,

"You must be smart at this." Other students were praised for their effort: "You must have worked really hard." Why just a single line of praise? "We wanted to see how sensitive children were," Dweck explained. "We had a hunch that one line might be enough to see an effect." Then the students were given a choice of test for the second round. One choice was a test that would be more difficult than the first, but the researchers told the kids that they'd learn a lot from attempting the puzzles. The other choice, Dweck's team explained, was an easy test, just like the first. Of those praised for their effort, 90 percent chose the harder set of puzzles. Of those praised for their intelligence, a majority chose the easy test. The "smart" kids took the cop-out."[4]

Praising *effort* motivated children to challenge themselves with harder work. Praising the child's *innate intelligence or results they achieved* seemed to encourage children to take little risk, avoiding the harder puzzles.

Praise of intelligence created a fear of failure and lessened a child's willingness to attempt a harder test. This is the exact opposite of what parents want to see in their children—a perfect example of the "Inverse Power of Praise" at work.

Other researchers have come to the same conclusion about the potential negative effect of praising the *person* rather than the *person's effort*. Psychologists Kyla Haimovitz and Jennifer Corpus studied college students at Reed college with a similar study design as Dr. Dweck.

The college students were divided into two groups and given praise for solving puzzles. Upon completion, one group was given praise for the effort they gave the challenge ("praising the process") and the second group was praised for their intelligence ("praising the person").

As in previous studies, Drs. Haimovitz and Corpus found that praising effort motivated the students to try to continue with more challenging puzzles whereas praising intelligence seemed to make these college students less willing to continue on to more challenging puzzles.[5]

Making Sense of the Data: How does this research relate to parenting and our case of Katherine?

Common sense tells us that praising a child for a behavior makes that behavior more likely to be repeated, especially if that praise comes from the most significant person in their life—their parents. But when the majority of the praise is directed at telling the child how intelligent, beautiful, athletic, or awesome they are, it will eventually make the child less likely to put forth effort and risk experiencing a failure.

No child wants to disappoint their parents, especially if that disappointment means having the praise cease. Additionally, at some point the child realizes that their parents' view of their performance does not coincide with the rest of the world's vision of them. The reality of the child's day-to-day experience with their peers and teachers quickly reveals to older children that they might not be as special and talented as their parents believe them to be.

Eventually, these children realize that their parents' expectations are unreasonable. And this creates a situation where the child has a heightened fear of failure and a reluctance to try new tasks which may lead to disappointment and disillusionment.

This sequence of events is exactly what happened to Katherine in the example that opened this chapter. Even though Katherine's parents hoped to increase her self-esteem and confidence by making Katherine believe that she was ultra-talented and beautiful, the end result was the exact opposite. Unrealistic praise crippled Katherine's motivation and effort.

When the majority of the praise is directed at telling the child how intelligent, beautiful, athletic, or awesome they are, it will eventually make the child less likely to put forth effort and risk experiencing a failure.

How do experts suggest parents use praise as a positive force for children?

How should parents use praise with their children? Good guidance comes from Jennifer Henderlong Corpus and Mark Lepper, psychologists who have analyzed over 30 years of studies on the effects of praise (Henderlong and Lepper 2002). They determined that praise can be a powerful motivating force if you follow these guidelines:

- Be sincere and specific with your praise
- Praise kids only for traits they have the power to change
- Use descriptive praise that conveys realistic, attainable standards
- Be careful about praising kids for achievements that come easily
- Be careful about praising kids for doing what they already love to do
- Encourage kids to focus on mastering skills—not on comparing themselves to others[6]

Why do some parents use praise excessively?

All parents see their children as special and unique. This is only natural. Parents fall in love with their children and that love often makes it difficult to see their children's talents objectively. I think every parent struggles with objectively evaluating their own children, but I believe that certain factors within the family can make clear-eyed objectivity more difficult to achieve.

The most obvious of these factors is a family having just one child. In this situation, all the parental love and attention are focused on one child. It's easy to see how parents can indulge in excessive praise and admiration for their one-and-only.

I have also noticed that parents who wait until closer to the end of their reproductive life to have children often have more difficulty not giving excessive praise to their children. Maybe this has something to do with the parents' realization that due to their advanced age, they have less time to spend with their offspring.

Finally, I have noticed that parents who tend to struggle with anxious mood and low self-esteem are more likely to have more difficulty seeing their children objectively, setting reasonable goals for them, and not praising excessively. I can only guess at the basis of this behavior, but I suspect that inflating the child's abilities somehow helps the parent cope with their mood difficulties.

Could it be that an excessive praiser is trying not so much to influence their *child's* self-esteem but rather convince *themselves* of how special their child is? Is the praise directed at changing the child's behavior or attitude or is it to immunize a parent from disappointment?

An extreme form of parental anxiety that interferes with a parent's ability to see their child objectively was described in 1964 by a prominent pediatrician named Dr. Morris Green. Dr. Green noticed that parents whose child had an illness early in life (an illness that the parent *perceived* as life-threatening) often went on to have great difficulty not becoming overprotective of the child, setting normal behavioral limits, or seeing the child objectively.

He coined this situation the "Vulnerable Child Syndrome."[7] Many of the children who developed this syndrome really only had very minor illnesses, but their parents saw things differently. They were convinced that the illness was life-threatening and critical.

The child's illness seems to have triggered an exaggerated anxiety response in the child's parents, that persisted long after the health crisis had abated. From that point on, this child's parents saw them as vulnerable and more fragile than other children.

In all of these situations, excessive praise and unrealistic perceptions of a child may be the result. Children raised in the households Dr. Green described (with a heightened sense of vulnerability of the children) turn out to show more need for medical care during their childhoods and exhibit more behavioral difficulties than children raised by parents without these anxieties.[8]

What are the barriers to the proper parental use of praise?

Why do parents become excessive praisers? I believe it's for one of three reasons:

- To inflate the child's self-esteem in an attempt to boost the child's confidence.

- To create a positive perception of their child in their own mind.

- To cover up some severe anxiety that the parent carries about their child experiencing failures and vulnerabilities.

Suggestions for using praise effectively with your children

I believe that parents can avoid the difficulties associated with excessive praise by being conscious of the following situations:

- Being aware that excessive and poorly used praise can have the opposite effect that a parent wants, *reducing* a child's confidence instead of *increasing* it.

- Recognizing that parental anxiety and insecurity can lead many parents to use excessive praise with their children.

- Resisting the trend among parents and child psychologists that encourage the promotion of self-esteem by praising children frequently.

- Avoiding the tendency to thrust children into hyper-competitive activities and pursuits when they are young.

- Recognizing that some failure is your child's *best teacher* in life. Make sure you avoid the tendency that so many parents have of shielding their children from the natural consequences of defeat, failure, and disappointment as they are growing.

What do you do if you recognize that you are not using praise effectively?

We all know that children don't come with instruction manuals, and new parents aren't bestowed with a psychology degree on their way home with their newborn babies. But parenting is a journey, and learning to adapt your parenting to maximize your *positive influence* on your children is one of the most important tasks you will have in your life.

I know you want to do your best at getting it right. So, take a few minutes and think about how you are using the tools in your toolbox to guide your children toward becoming a Great Kid. Are you leading by example, allowing your older children to experience the consequences of their actions, allowing them to learn from their failures, setting reasonable expectations for their achievements, and of course, using praise and punishments effectively?

If you conclude that you are *praising the person* (attributes that your child cannot control like looks or intelligence) rather than *praising the process* (your child's hard work, perseverance, focus) make a course adjustment immediately! Change the direction of the USS Family for smoother sailing. We want your children to become Great Kids and then graduate to becoming hard-working, resilient, happy adults.

Here are some things I want you to consider if your use of praise and other parenting tools may be suboptimal:

- Realize that you may be harming your child.
- Realize your praise may have the opposite effect of what you intended.
- Do a check and make sure you are using praise effectively.

Start by asking yourself the following questions:

- Do I give out praise very often with my child? Could this be from *my need* for my child to be exceptional?
- Am I the kind of parent who allows my child to experience the natural consequences of actions, or am I a rescuer?
- Am I uncomfortable with my child experiencing failure? Do I avoid it at all costs?
- Am I uncomfortable with my child experiencing disappointment?
- Am I praising talent or effort?
- Do I see my child as more vulnerable than other children?

After answering these questions, if you conclude you are not using praise effectively, commit to improving. Get help if needed, or simply develop some rules about using praise. The list I presented earlier in this chapter would be a good place to start. Using praise effectively is fundamental to raising emotionally healthy, motivated, and psychologically resilient children.

Use Praise Effectively.

Parents need to learn how to properly use praise and consequences to guide their children to becoming Great Kids. You are your child's greatest advocate. I certainly believe this to be true. But excessive praise, especially praise for traits that the child has no control over, can be counterproductive.

Trying to convince a child that they are cut from cloth they were not will do them a disservice. Instead of heaping unrealistic praise on a child in hopes they will feel good about themselves, parents should mete out praise only when their child has exerted a strong effort toward a worthy goal. Praise the process (effort, determination, persistence) not the person (traits a child cannot control).

Now You Know

- Praise used indiscriminately with children can have the opposite effect of what is intended by parents. This is known as the "inverse power of praise."
- Excessive praise can make a child averse to trying hard tasks.
- Excessive praise can lower a child's self-esteem.
- Excessive praise can give a child an unrealistic perception of their own abilities.
- Parents should praise effort not achievement.
- Parents should avoid praising traits for which a child has no control.
- Praise should only be given when it is earned.
- Overly anxious or insecure parents often use praise ineffectively.

What Can You Do?

1. Realize that poor use of praise and consequences can harm your child.
2. Try to avoid situations where you tend to use excessive praise. (See list on preceding page.)
3. Make a realistic appraisal of your use of praise and consequences. If you conclude there is a problem, commit to change.
4. Realize that if you as a parent need help, ask for it.
5. Don't hesitate to use natural consequences as an effective teacher for your children.

3

Good Parenting Involves Consistent Boundaries

"Nothing changes behavior like consequences," or its corollary, "The school of natural consequences teaches AP Life."

—Doc Smo *Pearl*
Portable Practical Pediatrics Podcast
May 5, 2015

"Kids will eventually respect parents who are honest, committed to their well-being, and who set reasonable limits for them."

—Doc Smo *Pearl*
Portable Practical Pediatrics Podcast
June 5, 2010

The Story of Logan:

By most measures, Logan seemed to be a bright 14-year-old with a wonderful childhood. His parents had a stable marriage and enjoyed an above-average income. The family lived in a single family home in an area of town with good schools. Logan's dad was stably employed as an insurance agent. His mom was an elementary school teacher. Logan had a sister three years his junior. By all accounts from friends and family, Logan's family had it all—stability, emotionally healthy parents, active parental involvement, and parents whose expectations of Logan were reasonable.

Yes, everything in Logan's family was good except for one thing: his parents had trouble setting limits with respect to his behavior. Logan's mother found it difficult to deny him things because she desperately wanted him to love her. His father, on the other hand, just found conflict and emotional outbursts with Logan very unpleasant. He avoided them at all costs. Crying and tantrums were Logan's secret weapons to get what he wanted or to avoid what he didn't want. The end result was a strong reluctance to tell Logan, "No."

When Logan was young, his parents' distaste for conflict manifested as a lot of begging. They would plead, "Logan, please don't do that." Logan was never really told that he had to obey his parents, share his toys with his sister, or follow the house rules. Gradually, Logan began to realize that none of his parents' demands were actually demands. They were more like requests that he could follow if he wished. It didn't take Logan long to learn to object to his parents' wishes in a vocal manner. When it was time to turn the TV off and go to bed, there was always refusal or a tantrum on Logan's part and acquiescence by his parents.

As you might expect, eventually Logan's parents solved his bedtime struggles by putting a TV in his room for him to use as he wished. Additionally, when Logan refused to eat the meal his family was consuming, his parents fixed him a special dinner of his liking. While out shopping with his family, if Logan was denied a toy he saw and fancied, he would have a full-blown temper tantrum. Of course, this kind of display of emotion got him the toy, no questions asked. Logan turned out to have more toys than he could possibly ever play with. Sadly, Logan saw himself as an adversary of his parents. Resistance was his first instinct to any limit they tried to impose. He had little reason to want to please his parents and was quick to pull the trigger of refusal.

By the time Logan became a teen, he had learned to be in total control of his family. Logan routinely refused to obey his parents' curfews and other restrictions they attempted to impose. Rather than tantrums being his weapon of defiance, he now simply ignored his parents' requests or became physically threatening—especially with his mother.

Logan became an out-of-control teen with no prospects of this changing. His parents unfortunately realized that they had failed in creating and using their parental authority. They saw how other parents were able to make and enforce limits for their teens, but somehow they were unable to do so. Logan's teen years put his family under a lot of stress, eventually ending in his parents' divorce.

A Pediatrician's Perspective of Logan and His Family

Logan's story is a sad but common saga that pediatricians see unfold all the time. Logan's parents were ambivalent about setting and enforcing limits for him as soon as he was born. You can see that theme running throughout the story of his childhood—from his disorganized bedtime in infancy and childhood, to his unhealthy "rigid" diet, to his out of control teenage years.

Despite being born into a family with many advantages, Logan spent much of his emotional energy struggling with issues of control, rebelling against any limitations that his parents tried to set for him. Why was accepting authority so difficult for Logan, you ask? I can only surmise an answer to this question, but I believe a strong component was his parent's reluctance to use their parental authority to set and enforce reasonable limits for him.

Pediatricians get a quick and strong sense of this when watching how new parents cope with the challenging tasks that infants and toddlers present to their parents. I was worried that Logan's parents were heading for a difficult time by the time Logan had reached his first birthday.

In this chapter, we will explore and discuss the vital parental task of limit-setting. Children start out life totally self-centered and instinctively resisting any kind of limitations. Good parenting, the kind that leads to the raising of Great Kids, mandates that parents learn to use their parental authority to enforce age-appropriate rules and limitations on their children.

Those parents that struggle with this parenting task often end up with children who have trouble moving from the "me" stage to the "we" stage. If parents don't cultivate a parenting style that allows them to lovingly enforce limits on their children, ending up with a Great Kid becomes much more unlikely.

Exploring the power parents have to discipline (create limits for) their children

I believe (and have observed) that a child's ultimate adult personality is, to a large degree, shaped by his or her parents. Certainly a child's personality has biological roots as well, as we will discuss in Chapter 6. But for now, I am going to limit this discussion to the impact of parenting.

In this chapter, we will explore how parents' use (or lack of use) of their *parental authority* configures and shapes their child's ultimate personality. "What is parental authority?" you may be asking. It's the ability that parents acquire to impose limits on their children.

Parents possess parental authority through an understanding between them and their child. This understanding is that the parents have the right to completely control the child's behavior, as long as those limits are reasonable and based in love.

Parental authority gives parents the right to set a bedtime for their children, insist that they eat good food, take a bath periodically, brush their teeth, stay out of the street, stay away from friends who are deemed unruly, do their homework, respect the word of adults, etc.

Think of parental authority as an unwritten contract between parents and children that gives parents most of the power. You can already see that Logan, the child I presented in the vignette at the beginning of this chapter, wasn't subscribing to the contract. No way, no how. More on Logan in a few minutes.

Defining discipline and parental authority

Let's start by defining the word discipline as it relates to parenting. The word "discipline" originates from the Latin word *disciplina* which means "instruction" and derives from the root *discere* which means "to learn."

Ask most parents what the word discipline means, and chances are you will hear descriptions of various types of punishment, not instruction. In the context of contemporary parenting, disciplining is synonymous with punishment.

But if you think about it, shaping a child's behavior involves rewards, punishments, setting limits, managing consequences for the child, and leading by example. When parents use all of these tools, you can see that the word discipline comes closer to its original Latin root meaning of instruction.

These are the tools that parents have to work with to cultivate that Great Kid that everyone wants. Children learn to conform to social normative standards by having their behavior praised when appropriate, negatively critiqued when it is out of boundaries, having clear limits set, experiencing the consequences of their actions, and having appropriate behavior modeled for them by their parents.

It seems obvious, but during your parenting journey don't forget this Doc Smo pearl: *"You are the parent and they are the child... play your part."* Or this little gem of a pearl from my blog/podcast, *"Making the babies was the easy part of parenting."*

Now on to officially defining the concept of "parental authority." Psychologists and the legal community have coined this term to describe a fundamental duty of parents—to impose limits on their children's behavior and to teach them socially acceptable behavior.

Parental authority is a right and an obligation that parents possess simply by being a child's parent. It comes with the birth process, no application or license needed. But if a parent (or parents) refuses to accept and use their parental authority (as in the case of Logan) they are likely to have difficulties steering their child toward healthy psychological development and may even be considered neglectful parents in the eyes of the law.

On the other hand, should a parent or parents use harsh methods of exercising their parental authority, they are setting up their child for a different type of maladaptive personality problem and risk being abusive.

Clearly, use *too little* or *too much* parental authority, and parents put themselves and their child at risk of getting off track toward becoming a Great Kid. Parents need to learn to thread the needle when it comes to the use of parental authority.

All parents are forced to discipline, impose limits, and teach self-control.

Limit setting and disciplining children, with the goal of teaching them self-control, are not duties that parents can abdicate. Parents have to shift their child from the "me" state of mind that we were all born with toward the "us" mindset.

I can't emphasize how important this task is for parents. Next to food, shelter, and protection, this is a primary duty of parenting. When parents fail at their limit-setting duties, children are bound to suffer. Parents who underuse or overuse their parental authority set their child up for long-term problems that we are about to explore.

Let's start by looking at the two extremes of the use of parental authority—too little or too much—by going down one of my favorite places, Science Drive.

Parents have to shift their children from the "me" state of mind that we were all born with toward the "us" mindset.

"A Detour Down Science Drive"—Parenting Styles

The study of parenting styles and their effects on children was pioneered by a young clinical psychologist, Dr. Diana Baumrind. She studied and worked at UCLA Berkeley. Her research, dating back decades, revolutionized our understanding of parenting styles and childhood outcomes.

The data Dr. Baumrind collected dates back to the 1960s but has held up to the test of time. She literally invented and defined the study of parenting styles. Her research has been widely studied and quoted for decades, and it is as relevant today as it was when she wrote it—especially from a pediatrician's view. Here is a brief synopsis of her 50 years of research. It is fundamental to understanding what parents can do to produce a Great Kid.

Dr. Baumrind's Classification of Parenting Styles

Authoritative parents

The authoritative parent attempts to direct the child's activities in a rational, issue-oriented manner. She encourages verbal give and take, shares with the child the reasoning behind her policy, and solicits his objections when he refuses to conform. Both autonomous self-will and disciplined conformity are valued by the authoritative parent. Therefore, she exerts firm control at points of parent-child divergence but does not hem the child in with restrictions. She enforces her own perspective as an adult, but recognizes the child's individual interest and special ways. The authoritative parent affirms the child's present qualities, but also sets standards for future conduct. She uses reason, power, and shaping by regime and reinforcement to achieve her objectives and does not base her decisions on group consensus or the individual child's desires.

Authoritarian parents

The authoritarian parent attempts to shape, control, and evaluate the behavior and attitudes of the child in accordance with a set standard of conduct, usually an absolute standard, theologically motivated and formulated by a higher authority. She values obedience as a virtue and favors punitive, forceful measures to curb self-will at points where the child's actions or beliefs conflict with what she thinks is right conduct. She believes in keeping the child in his place, in restricting his autonomy, and in assigning household responsibilities in order to inculcate respect for work. She regards the preservation of order and traditional structure as a highly valued end in itself. She does not encourage verbal give and take, believing that the child should accept her word for what is right.

Permissive parents

The permissive parent attempts to behave in a non-punitive, acceptant, and affirmative manner toward the child's impulses, desires, and actions. She consults with him about policy decisions and gives explanations for family rules. She makes few demands for household responsibility and orderly behavior. She presents herself to the child as a resource for him to use as he wishes, not as an ideal for him to emulate, nor as an active agent responsible for shaping or altering his ongoing or future behavior. She allows the child to regulate his own activities as much as possible, avoids exercise of control, and does not encourage him to obey externally defined standards. She attempts to use reason and manipulation, but not overt power, to accomplish her ends.[1]

Neglectful parents

This is a classification used in subsequent studies done after Dr. Baumrind's original classification. The neglectful parent demonstrates low responsiveness to her child's feelings and emotional needs and, at the same time, is also low on demandingness.

Dr. Baumrind and other psychologists have broken down these parenting styles into different elements that we can find summarized in the following grid:

Parenting Styles

	Responsiveness (High)	Responsiveness (Low)
Demandingness (High)	Authoritative Parent Style	Authoritarian Parent Style
Demandingness (Low)	Indulgent/ Permissive Parent Style	Neglectful Parent Style

The core features that distinguish Dr. Baumrind's descriptions of parenting styles are demandingness and responsiveness. These terms speak for themselves. An "authoritarian parent" uses a large amount of demandingness and control of their children without a lot of sensitivity to their child's emotions. An authoritarian parent is low on responsiveness and empathy for their child's feelings. Studies have shown that this lack of parental sensitivity seems to alter the child's personality development.

Personally, I see the authoritarian parenting style as using overly harsh parental authority— more than most children require. Think about it. It is very difficult for a child to learn to control their own emotions and self-control when they are under the yoke of heavy demands being imposed by parents who are not very emotionally responsive to their feelings. Dr. Baumrind and other psychologists are not fans of the authoritarian parenting style, and their research tends to associate poor outcomes with these families.

The "permissive parent," like Logan's, is low on demandingness but high on responsiveness. Recall that Logan's parents made few demands on him. At the same time, they were overly sensitive to his feelings and reactions. This combination of factors allowed Logan to essentially be in control of his parents— clearly a bad state of affairs.

This parenting style tends not to produce children with the strongest personalities or best behaviors. In the case of "permissive parenting," parents have failed to accept and use their parental authority for whatever reason. Unfortunately, I see this kind of parenting all the time, especially among the affluent families that I care for.

Another parenting style that psychologists define has been coined "neglectful." This style of parenting was not part of Dr. Baumrind's original description, but was added later. It is characterized by parents who are neither high on demandingness nor particularly responsive toward their children. Again, the neglectful parenting style (like the authoritarian and permissive) does not produce the highest proportion of Great Kids.

Fortunately, there is a magic formula of demandingness and responsiveness that seems to hit the right balance. Dr. Baumrind called these parents "authoritative parents."

You can tell from her description that she felt these parents used the best style when it came to balancing their use of parental authority and being sensitive to their children's emotions.

Listen to the adjectives Dr. Baumrind used when describing the authoritative parent:

1. She is rational (i.e., non-emotional) when making parenting decisions.

2. She is willing to use verbal give-and-take with her children.

3. She is not overly restrictive with her children.

4. She sets high standards for their achievement and behavior.

5. She uses reason to shape her children's opinions.

All of these descriptors sound very positive to me, downright Mary Poppins-like. Not only did Dr. Baumrind find this to be the most successful parenting style, but subsequent research has confirmed her findings. To me, this discovery aligns with common sense. Parents who have high (but achievable) expectations of their children and are sensitive to their children's emotional needs are bound to raise children that have the most respect for their parents and are more likely to try to please their parents.

The Best Parenting Style, Confirmed.

The authoritarian style has consistently been associated with the best outcomes in childhood. Her research supports a fact that I summarized on my blog in the following Doc Smo pearl: "If you treat your children like adults, they may surprise you and act like one."

In 1991, Dr. Baumrind put her theory of parenting styles to the test with a relatively small group of children and parents. She found that while highly competent children (what I call Great Kids) could come from any of the parenting styles, the style that most consistently produced competent, confident, capable children was the authoritative parent style.[2]

In 1994, Dr. Baumrind's theory of parenting styles was again put to the test in a large study of children by a separate group of psychologists in California and Wisconsin. In this study, Steinberg et al., examined the behavior, school achievement, mental health, and psychosocial development of 2300 children in relation to the parenting style of the families in which they were raised.

Dr. Baumrind's theories were truly put to the test in this large study. The results confirmed that Dr. Baumrind was correct— different parenting styles produce children with different outcomes.

The worst outcomes were seen in the group of parents described as neglectful parents who showed little emotional responsiveness and little demandingness toward their children. The data confirmed that having high standards, demanding achievement, and at the same time being sensitive to a child's emotions and feelings is the sweet spot for parents and gives parents the highest chance of producing a Great Kid.

These psychologists concluded that the most independent, highest academic achieving children with the fewest emotional difficulties came from the group of parents who used the authoritative parenting style of demanding and warm.

Take a minute and recall the best teachers you ever had, the ones who really motivated you to put your best effort forward. *What were the characteristics that made them such an effective teacher other than a firm grasp and enthusiasm for their subject?*

My guess is that you noticed that they had high standards for their students, they consistently expected your best, they praised effort and not innate qualities about you, and at the same time were kind, sensitive and engaged to your feelings.

Even though they were demanding and expected a lot of you, they could be trusted to treat you fairly. You knew they had your best interests in mind and were emotionally invested in your success.

These are all the essential features of good parents, and this is the parenting style that leads to the best outcomes for children. In Dr. Baumrind talk, this is the essence of the demanding but warm authoritative parent.

Making Sense of the Data: How does this research relate to parenting and our case of Logan?

Let's get back to the story of Logan. Unfortunately, I have known far too many Logans during my pediatric career. As I see it, despite being lovely people with the best of intentions, Logan's parents are a good example of "permissive parents." They exhibit the combination of demanding very little from Logan while at the same time being overly responsive to his emotions. I believe that Logan's parents' permissiveness extended directly from their inability to set consistent, age-appropriate limits for his behavior. This is a problem that all permissive parents have.

It is generally accepted that permissive parents are more prone to produce children that are less successful, less resilient, and less responsible. This has been my experience as well. These children tend to have poor self-discipline skills, and their motivation and achievement tend to be low.

I can't tell you how many children I have seen whose parents were ineffective limit-setters for their children and whose kids turned out to have low life-goals and achievement despite being blessed with many of life's advantages. These children are often not able to take advantage of their opportunities because of lack of drive.

I believe this is a direct result of poor limit-setting, a lack of demandingness, and possibly poor use of praise by their parents. They simply lack self-control, the ability to think of the feelings of others, and motivation.

> *Becoming a disciplined, focused, motivated adult who is able to work with others doesn't just happen. As the title says, Great Kids Don't Just Happen—they are cultivated and nurtured by parents throughout their childhood.*

Becoming a disciplined, focused, motivated adult who is able to work with others doesn't just happen. As the title says, *Great Kids Don't Just Happen*—they are cultivated and nurtured by parents throughout their childhood.

Learning to work hard toward goals, overcome disappointment and failure, cooperate and compromise with others, and see the world through the eyes of others are things that children of permissive parents have trouble doing. This is because permissive parents allow their children to receive reward without effort.

This is just not how the adult world works. And that explains why so many of these children have trouble when they experience demands as they move into the adult world. Logan is certainly a good example of someone who had this difficulty.

Television legend, Fred Rogers, reflects on discipline and limit setting for children.

There is no doubt that Fred Rogers, the PBS children's television star, understood the children in his audience. Millions of children and parents watched his show for almost a half century. He was an important figure and a household name from 1968-2001.

A soft-spoken Presbyterian minister by training, he had a way of connecting with children of all ages.

Rogers mastered the art of talking to young children on a level and tone that appealed to them. He recorded an amazing 895 episodes before he retired from television in 2001. He was so successful because he had a very good sense of what children need—interesting subjects, effectively presented in a predictable and entertaining manner, that taught them something about life.

His shows dealt with topics that were important to children. For example, how to understand one's own feelings and the feelings of others. And also accepting and embracing the concept of right and wrong, and empathy for others. He was truly a source of wisdom for both children and parents. His appearances and remarks in front of Congress are still legendary to this day. (https://www. americanrhetoric.com/speeches/fredrogerssenatetestimonypbs. htm) Listen to how important Mr. Rogers thought effective discipline was for children:

> Disciplining a child includes making rules. I prefer to think of this parenting task as "setting limits." It can be very frightening for a child not to have limits. Not only can the world outside be frightening, but the world inside, the world of feelings, can also be scary when you're not sure you can manage those feelings by yourself.[3]

Do you hear the theme of demanding but warm that Dr. Baumrind pioneered? I don't think Mr. Rogers knew of Dr. Baumrind, but they seemed to have come to the same conclusion about how to produce Great Kids. I am pretty sure that Dr. Baumrind would not approve of Logan's parents' approach with him, and I am fairly sure that Mr. Rogers wouldn't either.

What behaviors warn of parental trouble with limit-setting?

Let's look at some common difficulties of childhood through the lens of poor limit-setting. As a pediatrician, I am often involved in the fallout of parental inability to effectively set limits for their children. The trouble usually begins early, with an infant who has not become independent at night by a year of age. That comment may not sit well with many parents, but it is just what I have observed.

I know there are differences of opinion about sleeping expectations and arrangements during infancy, but I have observed that parents who struggle with sleep training and setting bedtimes for their children often have trouble with other limit-setting scenarios in childhood.

Getting an infant adjusted to going to bed at a set time and place is *the first* limit-setting task most parents encounter. Trouble here can indicate ambivalence about setting any limits and may predict trouble with future limit-setting.

Here is another common limit-setting hurdle for many parents today; the child who insists on eating a poor quality (albeit delicious) diet with a limited selection of nutritious foods. Parents often consult their child's pediatrician about a child who lacks variety in their diet. I refer to these children as "rigid eaters." These are not children with developmental disabilities or an eating disorder but perfectly normal children who have chosen the pattern of rigid eating because it entails the diet they prefer.

Usually, this pattern of eating develops at about two years of age. That's when most children start exerting strong preferences in food. But with the rigid eaters, their insistence on eating just a few foods persists until their teenage years or beyond.

While the roots of the rigid eating behavior *can have its origins in many things*, I believe much of it is an extension of parents not being effective limit-setters with respect to food. It is unpleasant for a child to be presented with food that they don't find appealing and equally unpleasant for their parents to endure the food battles that are likely to ensue. But failing to insist that a child eat predominantly healthy food is a big mistake. And I believe it is often the result of poor limit-setting.

Here is another situation that pediatricians often encounter that *may* have its roots in poor limit-setting ability of the child's parents. Pediatricians practicing today are often consulted about a child who is not doing well in school for a variety of reasons. Many of these children are labeled as having **A**ttention **D**eficit **D**isorder, meeting the criteria set forth by experts. During my pediatric career, the number of children qualifying for this diagnosis has steadily risen.

While I do believe that there are a group of children who have a biologically based inability to sustain attention, I also see many children who carry the ADD diagnosis who have a lack of motivation and whose parents have learned to expect little effort from them.

The basis of these children's academic difficulties, rather than being a biologically based disorder, stems from an unwillingness of their parents to create and enforce a productive study environment for their children, such as removal of TV and other distractions from the child's home. This is found in combination with low expectations on the part of the child's parents.

Failure of parental limit-setting is at the root of many children's academic difficulties. When I ask these families about the learning environment that exists at home, I often find that these children have televisions and other screens in their bedrooms for ad lib use by the child. They also have an abundance of video games with far too much gaming time, poorly structured bedtimes, as well as a lack of time set out for doing academic work at home.

In my mind, each of these factors could be remedied by parents who are willing to set limits that we know will improve a child's cognitive ability. (Smolen, Paul. *Can Doesn't Mean Should: Essential Knowledge for 21st Century Parents.* Durham, NC, USA: Torchflame Books, 2015.)

Finally, we can't forget about those teenage years with respect to limit-setting failures. As a pediatrician, I see the results of this all the time. Failure to enforce reasonable curfews often results in late-night automobile tragedies. Failure of parents to demand high academic standards allows their teens to over-commit their time to sports or a part-time job. Helping a teen appropriately allocate their time by limiting some activities is another one of those parenting tasks I often see families struggle with.

And let's not forget about those parties where parents turn a blind eye to alcohol and marijuana use. Not only are they not setting limits for these children, but they are often facilitating the whole affair—an amazing lack of limit setting.

Parental Barriers to Limit-setting

Why do some parents have trouble setting boundaries for their children? What is at the root of this difficulty? As you might expect, there are many reasons for their resistance to accepting this responsibility, but here are some of the common ones I have seen in my pediatric practice:

1. Some parents find limit-setting so unpleasant, with its inevitable conflicts, that they simply avoid it whenever possible.

1. Many parents want desperately to be liked by their children. Disciplining, making demands, and limit-setting are the last things parents who have this mindset want to do.

2. Some parents have disagreements with the other parent or relatives. The family has difficulty supporting one another in day-to-day parenting decisions. This lack of agreement leads to inaction on the limit-setting front.

3. Some parents don't have the emotional energy that parenting requires. Having young children to care for is very difficult and taxing. Add the burdens of parenting on top of jobs and financial stress or mental illness, and having enough energy to enforce limits is just not possible.

4. I also see a fair number of families who have experienced divorce. The now-single parents have abdicated some of their parenting duties to pursue their own social life.

5. Finally, I see some parents who had chaotic or disadvantaged childhoods and simply didn't know how to structure their child's life in order to set healthy limits.

Now You Know

- An essential function of parents is to effectively set and enforce age-appropriate limits for their children.

- Mastering the judicious use of parental authority is an important skill for parents to acquire.

- Different parenting styles with regards to demandingness and responsiveness have been shown to produce children with different degrees of success.

- Psychologists believe that the parents who demand high standards but who, at the same time, are sensitive to their children's feelings have the best chance of raising a healthy child—what I call a Great Kid.

- The harsh use of parental authority has long-term negative psychological and physical consequences for children as they grow into adults and should be avoided at all costs.

- One of the best parenting tactics is to allow a child to experience the natural consequences of their behavior whenever possible.

- Discussions of limit-setting problems are often part of pediatric health supervisory visits.

If your parenting is falling short on limit-setting for any of these reasons, here are some practical suggestions to get things on track:

What Can You Do?

Before your children are born, discuss your childhood experiences with your partner and decide how you would like to tackle the issue of limit-setting. Being on the same page makes your job much easier.

1. Realistically evaluate whether you tend to be an authoritarian, authoritative, neglectful, or permissive parent. Strive to be authoritative, as defined by Dr. Baumrind, by making high-but-attainable expectations of your children while at the same time being sensitive and understanding of their emotions.

2. Allow your children to experience failure and learn from their mistakes—especially when they are young, and their mishaps are less likely to be catastrophic for their futures.

3. Mastering the role of parenting means effectively learning to use your parental authority. Think of Goldilocks with your rules—not too harsh but at the same time not too lenient.

4. Identify situations where you have difficulty setting age-appropriate limits and work on being ready in advance when these situations arise.

5. Try to *never* engage in any of the following behaviors as a parent:
   - Swear at your child
   - Humiliate your child
   - Intimidate your child with threats of violence
   - Threaten your child with abandonment
   - Hit your child

- Make your child feel unloved

6. **Take immediate action by seeking professional help if your child is being exposed to any of the following:**
   - A family member has a drug or alcohol problem
   - A family member has been found to be sexually abusive
   - There is a family member, living with your child, who suffers from major depression or mental illness

4

Cultivating a Healthy Emotional Environment

"The ultimate goal of childhood is to create a happy, self-sufficient adult."

Doc Smo *Pearl*
Portable Practical Pediatrics Podcast
June 7, 2010

The Story of Alexander:

Alexander joined his family through orphan adoption when he was nine months old. He was born in East Asia and cared for exclusively in orphanages until his adoption. His biological father was a factory worker, and his mother was mostly homeless, living on the streets.

Alexander's adoptive American parents were middle class, college educated, successful individuals. They had three biological children who were five, eight, and twelve years old when Alexander came into their household. After an adjustment period of a few months, Alexander was able to conform to the family's sleep and eating routines—although it took a lot of effort on his parents' part.

Like all babies, he required a lot of attention and care. He seemed happy enough and certainly had all of his needs met. During his infancy, he was reaching his developmental milestones, especially his motor milestones. His ability to move actually happened earlier than most children, maybe because he was a very active baby. He seemed to love to be in motion.

When he came to the office for his checkups, I could tell that his mother was very caring and attentive. She seemed to adore him, and the rest of the family appeared to love him as well.

When Alexander became a toddler, however, he started to become more aggressive and active than most toddlers. He demonstrated great difficulty in coming to the pediatrician between one to three years of age. His fearful screaming was deafening and unnerving. This situation is not all that unusual for toddlers, and his mother and I thought things would get better after age two, like it does for most children.

Not in Alexander's case, however. His wild behavior began to increase. Mom described a child who had very little impulse control when at home or in public. He became totally out of control during his health visits in his third and fourth years. He would hit his mother, hit his siblings, and scream at the top of his lungs for his entire pediatric visit—very age inappropriate. His mother said that this kind of behavior was not unusual at home and school as well. The usual methods that pediatricians use to interact with a frightened child just simply didn't work with Alexander.

By his fourth birthday, his mother and I agreed that Alexander and his family needed psychological help to manage his increasingly aggressive behavior and obvious hyperactivity. After a few visits to the psychologist, Alexander got a diagnosis of Reactive Attachment Disorder (RAD), a common diagnosis for children who were adopted from East Asia. It was well known that orphans often got very poor care early in life in some parts of the world, living in a very harsh and lonely environment. They were often deprived of caring, loving adults to attend to their needs. This had devastating effects on their personalities and future health.

Their deprivation early in life is thought to lead to their subsequent difficulties with attachment, modulation of their emotions, and behavioral difficulties later in life. As Alexander grew older, it was obvious to everyone that he had a severe emotional disorder. This disorder was likely caused by his early childhood experiences in infancy. As far as everyone could tell, his adoptive family was providing a wonderful environment in which for him to grow up.

The psychologists concluded that a poor emotional climate and a lack of secure attachment to caregiving adults very early in life seemed to have caused Alexander major mental health problems. As Alexander grew into adolescence, his emotional outbursts only grew worse, and his lack of self-control and judgment began to get him in trouble with the law.

My last contact with Alexander's family was an unpleasant one. His distraught, crying mother called to tell me that the juvenile court had sentenced Alexander to a residential facility for criminal offenders less than 18 years old. It seemed like Alexander, that cute baby from East Asia, with a wonderful adoptive family's love, was well on his way to a lifelong struggle with authority.

A Pediatrician's Perspective of Alexander and His Family

Unfortunately, I met a few Alexanders during my pediatric career. However, not all came from East Asia. We have homegrown Alexanders in America as well. The thing they all had in common was a very difficult, stressful infancy with inconsistent care by multiple caretakers.

You may have heard the saying, "A child's personality is formed in the first three months of life." This wisdom is an oversimplification but does point out that early infancy is a critical time when things can go wrong for children. Babies are especially sensitive to insecurity and a lack of nurturing during infancy. Without these things, their personalities can be permanently damaged.

And who is it that provides the security and nurturing for babies? An emotionally healthy mother or other consistent caretakers. So, you can see that anything that causes emotional distress in a baby's primary caretaker has the potential of damaging that baby in a very significant way. In this chapter, we are going to explore the effects of an unhealthy emotional environment on a child and offer suggestions for parents who need help on how to deal with this circumstance should it arise.

"A Detour Down Science Drive"—Effects of an Unhealthy Emotional Environment

The easiest way to see the effect that a poor emotional climate has on a young child is to consider one of the most extremely harsh emotional environments in which a child can be raised—that of institutional care. Much of the strongest evidence validating the critical nature of early parenting has come out of the orphanages of Communist Romania.

It is likely that Alexander, the young orphan that I just described, came from a similar institution. The horror of these places was only discovered by Western journalists in 1989, shortly after the iron curtain fell.

What the journalists saw was beyond disturbing and shockingly common. Under the Communist ruler Nicolae Ceausescu, women were forced to have at least five children by way of various government policies. The State needed workers, so the Romanian government placed a ban on abortions, imposed repressive taxes on childless women, and made birth control impossible to buy.[1]

The "state" needed children and was determined to get them—no matter the social cost or effect on its citizens. The result was an explosion of children being born to families who could not or did not want to care for them. Many of these children were abandoned and became wards of the state.

Eventually, a large number of these children ended up in state—run orphanages in an impoverished country with few resources. Here is how the Guardian magazine described the situation. "Motherhood became a state duty. The system was ruthlessly enforced by the secret police, known as the *Securitate*. Doctors who performed abortions were imprisoned, women were examined every three months in their workplaces for signs of pregnancy. If they were found to be pregnant and didn't subsequently give birth, they could face prosecution. Fertility had become an instrument of state control."[2] To say that the care of the children in these institutions was substandard or poor would be an extreme understatement. It was downright brutal and inhumane.

Journalists discovered infants tied to beds, receiving very little human contact. Older children were in straight jackets. Many children were starved and suffering from malnutrition. It was not unusual for many older children to spend the majority of their time in isolation.

The long-term psychological effects of institutionalization on children have gotten lots of study in the past few decades. Prominent among these researchers is Megan Gunnar, director of the Institute of Child Development at the University of Minnesota. Dr. Gunnar has collected a large database of children adopted from institutions around the world, and she has studied the effects of institutionalization on these children.

While every case is different, generally her research shows that institutional foster care has adverse effects on a child's brain.[3] Here is a summary of some of the features that institutionalized children exhibit.

Common Features of Young Children Raised in Institutions

- Smaller brains, especially prefrontal cortex
- Trouble with self-control and control of emotions
- Poorer memory
- Less cognitive flexibility
- More anxiety

Megan Gunnar PhD[4]

Fortunately, in the United States today, few children are raised in institutions when they are very young, but I include this information to give my readers a sense of how fragile young children are and how deprivation in a very young child can permanently change their lives.

Think about what an infant is desperately seeking—physical and emotional security from his or her caretakers. If all goes well, the bond formed between mom and infant is known as a "Secure Attachment." Without a secure attachment in place, all other aspects of personality development cannot happen. As we just saw from Dr. Gunnar's research, even the infant's brain development is altered. A lack of a secure attachment has devastating and long-lasting negative effects on an infant. Said another way, being raised in an emotionally healthy environment is absolutely fundamental if that child is to have normal brain and personality development.

Very few children in contemporary America suffer like the children did in Eastern Europe in those State run orphanages.

But common sense tells us that if extreme maltreatment, social isolation, or exposure to a poor emotional climate in infancy can do such profound damage to a young child, that milder forms of mistreatment may have similar, albeit milder, adverse effects.

Is there evidence that this is true? The answer to that question is a resounding, "Yes!" Let's explore milder and more subtle effects of a child growing up under the influence of an unhealthy emotional climate.

> *Being raised in an emotionally healthy environment is absolutely fundamental if that child is to have normal brain and personality development.*

Additional Evidence of the Negative Effect of a Poor Emotional Climate

We now know that a child does not have to be raised in an institution to suffer the negative effects of a suboptimal emotional climate because of some groundbreaking research by physicians at the Kaiser Health Foundation done back in 1995.

These adult physicians had a hunch that many of the chronic diseases that they were caring for in adults had their roots in these patient's childhoods. Their intuition turned out to be brilliant and right.

Proof came after these doctors collected data by administering a simple questionnaire to 17,000 of their participants over a two year period. This group of people (known as a cohort) was asked if they had experienced any of what they called "Adverse Childhood Experiences," also known by its eponym, "ACE factors." Here are the questions included in the Adverse Childhood Experience questionnaire.[5]

This survey was done in 2013.[6]

Adverse Childhood Experiences Questionnaire

Prior to your 18th birthday:

1. Did a parent or other adult in the household often or very often: Swear at you, insult you, put you down, or humiliate you? Or Act in a way that made you afraid that you might be physically hurt?

   _____Yes _____No (If yes, enter 1)

2. Did a parent or other adult in the household often or very often: Push, grab, slap, or throw something at you? Or Ever hit you so hard that you had marks or were injured?

   _____Yes _____No (If yes, enter 1)

3. Did an adult or person at least 5 years older than you ever: Touch or fondle you or have you touch their body in a sexual way? Or Attempt or actually have oral, anal, or vaginal intercourse with you?

   _____Yes _____No (If yes, enter 1)

4. Did you often or very often feel that: No one in your family loved you or thought you were important or special? Or Your family didn't look out for each other, feel close to each other, or support each other?

   _____Yes _____No (If yes, enter 1)

5. Did you often or very often feel that: You didn't have enough to eat, had to wear dirty clothes, and had no one to protect you? Or Your parents were too drunk or high to take care of you or take you to the doctor if you needed it?

   _____Yes _____No (If yes, enter 1)

6. Was a biological parent ever lost to you through divorce, abandonment, or other reason?

   _____Yes _____No (If yes, enter 1)

7. Was your mother or stepmother often or very often pushed, grabbed, slapped, or had something thrown at

her? Or Sometimes, often, or very often kicked, bitten, hit with a fist, or hit with something hard? Or Ever repeatedly hit over at least a few minutes or threatened with a gun or knife?

_____Yes _____No (If yes, enter 1)

8. Did you live with anyone who was a problem drinker or alcoholic, or who used street drugs?

_____Yes _____No (If yes, enter 1)

9. Was a household member depressed or mentally ill, or did a household member attempt suicide?

_____Yes _____No (If yes, enter 1)

10. Did a household member go to prison?

_____Yes _____No (If yes, enter 1)

Note questions 1, 3, and 13 deal with excessively harsh use of parental authority that created a very unhealthy emotional environment for this child. As you might expect, adolescents and young adults who exhibited trouble with impulse control and who exhibited criminal behavior at a young age were found by the Kaiser Permanente researchers to be far more likely to have these and other ACE factors in their childhoods when compared with control populations.

In fact, the authors concluded that there is a dose/response relationship between ACE factors and eventual criminal behavior; the more ACE factors a child endured, the higher their chance of criminal behavior!

If that is not proof that being raised in a household with poor emotional health isn't important, I don't know what is. Case closed in my mind. A poor emotional climate during childhood can be extremely damaging to a child's personality development as well as their long-term behavior and health.[7]

Researchers think they now know how being raised in an environment with ACE factors impairs the development of a child, especially a very young child under two years of age. We are all hard-wired to react to threats and life stresses, especially harsh stress like physical threats, by having the bodily reactions called the"fight or flight" responses. These physical responses involve increased cortisol and adrenaline levels, elevation in blood pressure and heart rate, and a host of other physiologic changes, all geared to get us ready to fight or run. (Hence the name "fight or flight".)

Babies and young children respond to physical and emotional threats with the same physiological responses as older children and adults. They react to separation from a caretaker, being yelled at, hit, or being physically threatened in the same way—with the fight or flight response. The problem comes when the stress or threat is not intermittent (as it is for most children) but becomes repetitive and chronic.

Children raised in these circumstances don't recover from this kind of chronic stress, and it begins to alter their basic physiology and brain development. This kind of chronic stress becomes very damaging and is given a different name: "toxic stress."

Strong evidence points to the fact that children raised in ACE-rich households show physiological signs of stress such as higher blood cortisol levels, higher adrenaline levels, a hormonal state that ultimately leads to an elevation in the body's inflammatory response (chronic inflammation), and abnormal emotional responses.[8] Unfortunately, all this carries into their adult lives.

Long-term Damaging Effects of Toxic Stress

Other studies have found that the effects of exposure to "toxic stress," (the term used for the impact of living in a household with ACE factors) in childhood extend beyond increasing a child's chances of developing behavior difficulties, mental illness, or criminal behavior.

Additionally, the risk of developing *serious adult chronic physical maladies* is significantly increased for these children. Just like with criminality, a dose-response relationship was found between exposure to ACE factors in childhood and the chance of developing adult physical chronic diseases such as hypertension, adult-onset diabetes, COPD, and alcoholism.

Look at this data collected by the CDC. Note the very broad range of diseases that these children suffered from (see chart below). Researchers have concluded that many adults with serious physical diseases developed these disorders because of things that happened to them when they were young! Many adult diseases are really *caused by toxic stress* that occurred when these adults were children—even before the children had memory of these traumas.[5]

ACES Can Have Lasting Negative Effects on Health and Well-Being

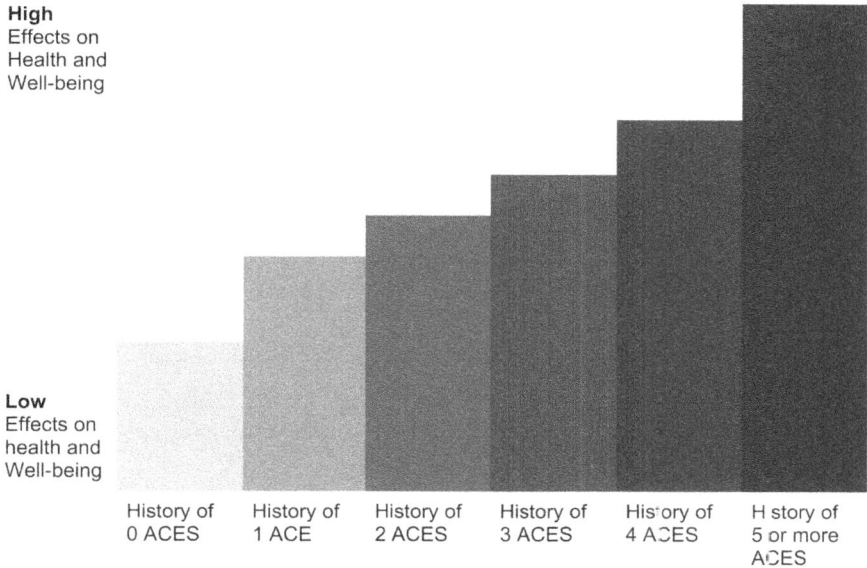

High
Effects on
Health and
Well-being

Low
Effects on
health and
Well-being

| History of 0 ACES | History of 1 ACE | History of 2 ACES | History of 3 ACES | History of 4 ACES | History of 5 or more ACES |

ACES have been found to have a graded dose-response relationship with 40+ outcomes to date (Data from CDC-Kaiser ACE Study 1998)

How commonly do children experience ACE factors?

Children growing up in homes with ACE factors happens far more commonly than you would think, as the data from the Kaiser Permanente group demonstrates.

The prevalence rates reflect the number of patients in the early cohorts of patients who experienced ACE factors in their first 18 years of life. You can see that approximately two thirds (63.9 %) of children grew up in a household with at least one ACE factor, with only about one-third (36.1%) growing up in a home with no ACE factors being present.

ACE Score Prevalence for CDC-Kaiser ACE Study Participants by Sex, Waves 1 and 2.

Number of Adverse Childhood Experiences (ACE Score)	Women Percent (N = 9,367)	Men Percent (N = 7,970)	Total Percent (N = 17,337)
0	34.5%	38.0%	36.1%
1	24.5%	27.9%	26.0%
2	15.5%	16.4%	15.9%
3	10.3%	8.5%	9.5%
4 or more	15.2%	9.2%	12.5%

Note: Research papers that use Wave 1 and/or Wave 2 data may contain slightly different prevalence estimates

What kind of health problems did these children have as adults?

What these researchers found was nothing short of shocking, unforeseen, and very disturbing. As I said before, the Kaiser cohort of adults with an array of chronic diseases was found to have had a much higher exposure to toxic stress and ACE factors than adults without chronic diseases. Just take a look at the variety of conditions from which they suffer:

- Alcoholism and alcohol abuse
- Chronic obstructive pulmonary disease
- Depression
- Health-related quality of life
- Illicit drug use
- Ischemic heart disease
- Liver disease
- Poor work performance
- Financial stress
- Risk for intimate partner violence
- Multiple sexual partners

- Sexually transmitted diseases
- Smoking
- Suicide attempts
- Unintended pregnancies
- Early initiation of smoking
- Early initiation of sexual activity
- Adolescent pregnancy
- Risk for sexual violence
- Poor academic achievement[8]

As you can see from this list, many of the effects of being raised in a poor emotional climate are psychological—manifesting as poor judgment, impulse control, and self-destructive behavior. The researchers expected to see adverse mental health among children raised with high ACE scores but were surprised at the additional strong association with serious *physical* diseases of adult life.

It is now generally accepted that being raised in a poor emotional climate is not just unpleasant; it can set a child on a disastrous course for the rest of their life, both mentally and physically.

By simply asking their patients about their childhood experiences and emotional climate in which they were raised, the Kaiser doctors discovered a strong link between adverse childhood experiences and both psychological and degenerative physical disorders.

What constitutes a healthy emotional environment?

We have had a look at what constitutes an unhealthy emotional environment and its terrible consequences for children. Now let's turn our attention to what we can learn on Science Drive about families who provide a healthy emotional environment for their children.

One of the largest (and certainly the oldest) studies of what makes humans live happy lives has come from data that studied a group of Harvard students dating back to 1938.

The study is called the Harvard/Grant Study, and it is the longest running longitudinal study of human development and happiness ever done. The study has collected data about the lives of a cohort of 268 male students for the past 75 years. And it continues to this day—even though only a few of its subjects are still living.

The idea was to find out what factors in a person's life lead to healthy aging, life success, and happiness. Data has been collected frequently by means of a questionnaire and analyzed periodically.

The fact that the Harvard/Grant study was done on the same people over such a long period of time has made it a powerful tool for studying happiness.

While numerous conclusions have been drawn from this data, the overarching theme that stands out from this research is that happiness in adult life is an extension of the closeness a child develops with his family, especially his mother. You just saw in the last section of this chapter how a *lack of a secure attachment* can devastate a child; now you are seeing how a healthy secure attachment helps a child throughout their life.

Said another way, a child raised in an emotionally healthy environment with a strong level of trust and attachment to their mother is more likely to lead a happy life and have healthy aging. It is the quality of the emotional environment a child experiences early in life that determines much of the happiness they will experience later in their life![9]

Other research from other sources has demonstrated how critical it is to be raised in an emotionally healthy environment *during the first few months of life*, exactly when Alexander was probably being shortchanged.

This fact is the basis of the statement you may have heard stating that a child's personality is formed in the first few months of life. Without an emotionally healthy environment from their parents early in life, healthy development and ultimate happiness is more difficult to achieve.

Happiness in adult life is an extension of the closeness a child develops with his family, especially his mother.

Other longitudinal studies have concluded the same thing as the Harvard/Grant Study.

Professor Richard Layard of the London School of Economics came to the same conclusion after he conducted a cohort/longitudinal study similar to the Harvard/Grant Study.

Professor Layard oversaw a study called the British Cohort Survey. His researchers have been following 9000 people, born in the United Kingdom over a three week period in 1970, by way of periodic surveys.

The study's authors concluded that the happiness of the people they studied had far more to do with their emotional health and stability both in childhood and adult life than to their academic or economic success. These are the exact same conclusions that the Harvard/Grant researchers came to.

Here are their conclusions in their own words:

> By far the most important predictor of adult life-satisfaction is emotional health, both in childhood and subsequently. Pro-social behaviour in childhood is the next most important childhood predictor. We find that the intellectual performance of a child is the least important childhood predictor of life-satisfaction as an adult. Intellectual performance is of course a good predictor of adult educational achievement and income.[10]

In their paper entitled *What Predicts a Happy Life?*, Dr. Layar et al. didn't measure the quality of the parent-child relationship like the researchers did in the Harvard Grant study, but I think the authors would agree that a healthy, stable relationship with one's parents in childhood is at the foundation of good mental health and happiness.[11]

Interestingly, high cognitive ability was a poorer predictor of happiness in adulthood than were emotional health and good conduct during childhood. Now we have two of the largest and oldest longitudinal studies demonstrating the same thing—the happiest adults are the ones that have good relationships with their parents during their childhoods.

Making Sense of the Data: Evidence shows that parenting matters.

I hope you are beginning to see that parenting matters a lot when it comes to raising a Great Kid. Let's take a moment to review our definition of a Great Kid that I presented earlier:

1. A young adult who is *self-sufficient*.
2. A young adult who can *maintain stable employment*.
3. A young adult who can create and *maintain long-term friendships and family relationships*.
4. A young adult who *lives without substance abuse dependency*.
5. A young adult who is *generally happy and emotionally stable*.
6. A young adult who can *abide by the laws of society*.

In Chapter 1, we explored the way parents use or misuse praise, and how it is an important determinant in their children's ability to withstand disappointment, have persistence in the face of difficulty, and be willing to work hard toward a goal.

I believe families using praise appropriately goes a long way towards producing children who ultimately become self-sufficient and are able to maintain stable employment—two of the six attributes of our Great Kid as an adult.

In Chapter 2, I presented information that I hope convinced you that setting age-appropriate limits throughout their childhoods while at the same time being emotionally sensitive to your children's feelings is the best parenting style to produce Great Kids.

It's my belief and experience that good limit-setting by parents is vital to achieving two other characteristics of a Great Kid: the ability to follow rules and laws and the avoidance of drug dependency.

Finally, in Chapter 3 I have presented you strong evidence that children who are raised in an emotionally healthy family are the ones most likely to achieve happiness and stability as adults—features three and five of a Great Kid.

Back to the story of Alexander

I think you can now see that Alexander and his adoptive parents were presented with tremendous obstacles to parenting success because of Alexander's early deprivation and lack of a secure attachment in infancy.

Institutions are not good places for babies. Infants need, above all else, to learn that those caring for them will protect them and be responsive to their needs, things that Alexander apparently did not get. No matter how wonderful and skillful his adoptive parents were, Alexander was already set on a difficult life course before he got started.

Good parenting is vital to producing the Great Kid every parent wants. I believe that the skill in which parents carry out the task of parenting is the single most important factor in determining their child's future—more important than the child's genetics, more important than a family's social status, and more important than the child's innate intelligence. I find this fact very encouraging since it means that parenting is at the core of a child's ability to become a Great Kid. Thank goodness parenting is something we have some control over.

The Parental Barriers that Interfere with the Ability to Create a Healthy Emotional Environment

It is said that parenting is the most difficult job most of us will ever have. This is true, since being successful at it requires such a sustained investment of a parent's time and energy. Twenty-four hours a day, seven days a week, year in and year out. That is why two parents in a household often fair better than when all the parenting is done by one.

But regardless of how many adults do the parenting, the child's needs must have priority. Parents who lack commitment to the task have a difficult time. Lack of emotional energy for the responsibility of being a parent is one barrier to creating a healthy emotional environment for children. Other life circumstances can also be very significant barriers:

- Untreated mental health problems that a parent has not confronted
- Substance abuse by parents
- Poverty, lack of education, and other suboptimal life circumstances
- The inability of some parents to ask for help

Finally, no discussion of a healthy emotional environment is complete with touching on the topic of corporal punishment with children. Unfortunately, many parents believe (because they were taught by their parents and society in general) that the frequent use of corporal punishment with their children is not only an acceptable method of discipline, but that it is vital to their learning rules and being obedient to adults. Nothing could be further from the truth.

In my experience, a parent's frequent use of violent spanking, more often than not, creates an unhealthy emotional environment and is a major barrier to healthy parenting.

One Family's Success

Trevor was born with a major birth defect involving his nervous system. For unknown reasons, his brain did not develop properly, and at birth, it was much smaller than expected. His parents weren't given much hope that Trevor would lead a normal life after his birth.

Trevor's family rolled up their sleeves and provided everything they could for him. As predicted by his medical specialists, he was slower at learning than his peers, but thanks to the encouragement of his family he was able to reach his full potential. Here's a quick list of things I think others can learn from Trevor's family:

- Encourage your child with physical healthcare needs to get out and play with their peers by helping them find adaptive ways to participate, or by signing them up for adaptive sports teams.

- Find the most appropriate school environment (within your financial means), even if that means changing districts or attending a special school. Encourage your child to join their same-age peers in activities like Sunday school, scouts, or other extra curricular activities. Help them live as normal a life as possible.

- Help your child work through emotional struggles and mental health issues. Help them be thankful for what they have, rather than focusing on limitations.

- Provide a healthy emotional climate by modeling how to process emotions, using good communication skills, balancing love with appropriate boundaries, and practicing positivity.

Resources for parents worried that their child has Reactive Attachment Disorder (RAD)

The National Child Traumatic Stress Network (NCTSN) www.nctsn.org. Funded by Congress, this is an organization that serves as a central hub to direct parents to resources available to help with families and children who have experienced or witnessed traumatic events. Excellent database of network participating facilities.

The Center for Family Development www.center4familydevelop.com. The website of a center in Western NY for the treatment of attachment problems run by a psychologist who is an expert in attachment problems. This is an educational website.

Zero to Three www.zerotothree.org. US based organization dedicated to promoting healthy parenting from birth to age three years. Mostly an information resource.

Center for Parent Information and Resources (CPIR) www.parentcenterhub.org. An organization dedicated to helping parents with children who have developmental problems. Emphasis is on early intervention services.

HelpGuide www.helpguide.org/articles/parenting-family/attachment-issues-and-reactive-attachment-disorders.htm. A website with articles devoted to helping parents with children who have mental health problems.

Heart to Heart Adoptions adoption.com/articles. A website designed to provide articles and resources to families with adopted children.

The Institute for Attachment & Child Development www.instituteforattachment.org. A treatment facility dedicated to RAD and children who have experienced early life trauma located in Colorado Springs, Colorado.

Now You Know

- "Emotional Environment/Climates" are terms that refer to how responsive a child's family is to their child's physical and emotional needs.

- It is clear that children raised in families with poor emotional environments are more likely to suffer major psychological and physical problems during their lives.

- A "secure attachment" refers to a child's emotional and physical comfort with their environment in infancy.

- A lack of formation of a secure attachment can have devastating consequences for a child's long-term emotional and physical well-being.

- Children raised in healthy emotional climates tend to be happier, healthier, and live longer than those without this influence during their childhoods.

- It is imperative for the well-being of their children that parents do everything possible to create a healthy emotional environment.

What Can You Do?

Replicate, as much as possible, Dr. Baumrind's "demanding but warm" parenting style. Avoid authoritarian, permissive, or neglectful parenting that we discussed earlier. Take a minute to go back into chapter 2 and review the characteristics of these parenting styles and make sure you know what you are shooting for.

1. Tell your children that you love them often. A family psychotherapist, Virginia Satir, famously said, *"We need four hugs a day for survival. We need eight hugs a day for maintenance. We need twelve hugs a day for growth."*

2. Always try and be empathetic toward your children. Listen to their feelings, and they will eventually learn to listen to yours and others.

3. If your family needs counseling or other help to achieve a good emotional climate, by all means, seek it.

4. Don't ignore mental health problems among your family members. Confront them head-on.

5. Mentor with parents who have been successful. Learn from other's successes. Friendships with other parents can be a very powerful tool to help during the inevitable difficult times as a parent.

6. Don't shield your children from experiencing failure. Accept the fact that some failure will help them grow, and let them learn from their failures while they are young.

7. Set *reasonable* expectations for your children and encourage and expect them to work hard.

5

Importance of a
Strong Parental Commitment

*"Parents create the reality
in which their children live."*

Doc Smo *Pearl*
Portable Practical Pediatrics Podcast
September 26, 2010

The Story of Devon:

Devon was born to a single mom who graduated from high school but had no other education. Devon's mom got by on some public assistance and a series of minimum wage jobs that offered no chance of advancement. Despite her lack of steady employment, she was a hard worker. With great struggle, she always managed to provide the basics for her three children.

The children's father provided very little help or support. In fact, the kids rarely had contact with their dad, who also struggled financially. Devon's dad lived in the same town but was only involved in the children's lives tangentially.

Despite working long and irregular hours, Devon's mom always managed to get him to school and help him complete his assignments when her help was needed. She got to PTA meetings, performances, and athletic events that Devon participated in. She was Devon's biggest fan—and his greatest critic!

Devon's mom thought nothing of correcting behavior she didn't like in public, even in front of his pediatrician. If his grades were poor, she made it clear that she expected more. But when he had success, Devon's mother was ecstatic. When he made the basketball team, she beamed with pride. When they came for their annual visits, I could tell that she adored Devon and expected big things from him. And he seemed to genuinely respect her, even though she was often unabashedly critical of him.

Devon graduated from high school with fairly good grades, a good attitude about life, and no fear of hard work. Consequently, he had many offers to attend college. His childhood had been full of disadvantages, but somehow Devon managed to thrive.

In my opinion, the reason for his success was sitting across from him at every visit to my office—his mother. Even though she had to do all the parenting by herself, she was a force he had to reckon with. Her presence in his life was palpable and constant. She was forceful when she needed to be, but at the same time she was extremely supportive and very sensitive to Devon's feelings.

She wanted better for Devon than she was able to achieve, and she was determined that he was going to get it. Devon had learned to see the world through his mother's eyes, and somehow, despite being raised in a community with lots of failure surrounding him, he was well on his way to becoming successful.

What made Devon different than many of his friends? He had a mother that demanded high standards, was sensitive to her son's feelings, and put a tremendous amount of her own effort toward his success. She was emotionally consistent and always present. In my mind, she epitomized a parent who has strong parental commitment.

Contrast Devon's story with that of Oliver.

The Story of Oliver:

Oliver started life with two parents, but soon that multiplied to four. His biological parents divorced when he was four years old, forcing him to bounce between two step-families that had joint custody. Oliver had multiple households, new parents, and a variety of siblings.

Oliver often felt displaced. He found it very difficult to go back and forth between his two families. His biological parents didn't fight outright, but Oliver was always aware of the tension between them. His allegiances would go back and forth between his blended families throughout his childhood.

Sometimes he was closer to his biological mother, and sometimes to his biological father. He was constantly asked to take sides. Throughout elementary school, Oliver often had stomach aches, headaches, and other non-serious disorders. He missed a lot of school and got marginal grades.

It was obvious that Oliver didn't put forth his best effort in regards to his school work. He was happy just getting by academically but graduated from high school nonetheless. His options for further education were limited by his poor grades, few skills, and low motivation.

A Pediatrician's Perspective of Devon, Oliver, and Their Families

I have seen many Olivers during my career. We probably all have known children like him. Overall, there is a sadness and hurt that these children carry, I believe mainly because of their life circumstances.

Their sadness then translates directly into physical and emotional difficulties. And I can see why. They never got *full* support from either parent. In Oliver's case, his basic needs were met, but like many blended families, his family life was full of instability and shifting allegiances. For Oliver, this impaired his ability to develop the way he might have had he not had extra stress.

Oliver's parents certainly loved him as much as any parent loves their children, but the chaos of their family life got in the way of that love being able to have its full, positive impact. This view of his childhood might seem harsh, but I think it is the reality of what many children experience.

His parents would probably say that they had no choice other than divorce. While that fact is probably true, I think it squelched Oliver's ability to reach his potential.

It was possible for Oliver's parents to give him the strong parental commitment that he needed, but their life circumstances made that difficult to do. Unfortunately, the healthy emotional environment discussed in Chapter 4 wasn't there for Oliver.

When we contrast Devon's one parent with Oliver's four, I think you can see that Devon got the better childhood. This was because of his mother's singular focus, energy, and devotion to his success. It is a perfect example of how strong parental commitment benefits children.

What is a strong parental commitment?

Let's break down what I mean by *strong parental commitment.* The Webster dictionary defines the word *commitment* in the following manner:

- a promise to do or give something

- a promise to be loyal to someone or something

- the attitude of someone who works very hard to do or support something[1]

Now, let's look at the definition of commitment in relation to being a parent. Embedded in the meaning of commitment is a promise to taking *strong action*, to *work very hard* on your child's behalf, to exhibit *unwavering loyalty* for your child, and to *publicly express* an attitude of support toward your child.

Think about the cases of Devon and Oliver in light of this definition. You can immediately see that Devon got the parent with the stronger parental commitment, because Devon's mom was always present in his life.

Skeptical of that perspective? Think about interviews with successful athletes after they have achieved some long sought out goal. Who do they almost always attribute their victories to? *That's right, a strong adult who committed themselves to the child's success during their childhood*—someone like Devon's mother.

Their coaches seem to come in a distant second in importance when the athlete discusses the reasons for their success. While the coaches taught them the intricacies and nuances of their sport, their parent(s), by committing to their child's long-term success, maximized their child's chances of obtaining an amazing achievement.

This is not only true for athletes; I believe it is true of all children. Children don't just become disciplined, kind, self-sufficient adults. All of us were born unskilled, uneducated, selfish, and undisciplined. It's that strong parental commitment to a child's success that molds them into self-sustaining, productive, happy adults.

> *Commitment is...a promise to work very hard on your child's behalf, a promise to exhibit unwavering loyalty for your child, and a promise to publicly express an attitude of support toward your child.*

"A Detour Down Science Drive"—Achieving Better Outcomes Among Disadvantaged Children

One of the best predictors of a child's success in life is the success (or lack thereof) that their parents were able to achieve during their own educational careers.[2] This only makes sense. If a child's parent had very little success during their school experience, maybe they have passed their negative attitude toward school down to their children.

Additionally, parents who struggled in school probably lack the skills to show their children how to be successful at academic pursuits. I have always thought that teachers are good at providing *information* to children, but parents are the ones that teach children how to organize, prioritize, and complete school assignments. Teachers provide facts, and parents provide motivation and the drive to succeed.

It is parents who are the driving force behind children who succeed in school by providing their commitment and expertise to the task of academic success. It really doesn't matter how intelligent a child is. Without the skills I just listed, and a parent's strong commitment, a child is unlikely to succeed in their academic career. And as we all know, with academic success usually comes upward social mobility, a higher income, and an easier life.

Every parent wants their children to succeed, but there is a big leap between wanting academic success and actually achieving it. What are the barriers that get in the way of parents being able to fulfill the role of a committed parent? Experts think that they know the answer to that question.

The Economic Policy Institute is a nonpartisan, nonprofit think tank composed mostly of economists. They have put considerable effort toward studying, identifying, and offering solutions to the obstacles standing in the way of success for disadvantaged children. Here are the five major disadvantages they have identified that can hold back academic performance of children raised in poverty:

1. **Parenting practices that impede children's intellectual and behavioral development:** Lower social class parents engage in fewer educationally supportive activities with young children, such as reading aloud or playing cognitively stimulating games. Lower social class parents also exert more direct authority and offer children fewer choices in their daily interactions, leaving them less prepared for "critical thinking" when school curricula starts to expect it. Parents' failure to engage in educationally supportive activities is associated with children's poorer academic and behavioral outcomes.

2. **Single parenthood:** Mothers raising children alone are more likely to be low-income and less educated. Their children typically have lower test scores, are more likely to drop out of school, and have greater emotional and behavioral difficulties (more delinquency and violence, more school dropout, more suicide).

3. **Parents' irregular work schedules:** Computerized scheduling and the weakening of norms governing employers' responsibility for employee welfare have combined to produce irregular work schedules for many hourly paid low-wage workers and the less educated. Unpredictable schedules make it difficult, if not impossible, to place children in high-quality child care centers and to establish regular home routines in which children can thrive. Children of mothers with non-standard schedules have worse verbal and other cognitive skills, mental health, and behavior.

4. **Inadequate access to primary and preventive health care:** Minority children and those whose parents are less educated or who live in low-income neighborhoods are less

likely to have personal physicians or nurse practitioners, or to receive necessary referrals to specialists. No research directly associates physician access with children's cognitive or non-cognitive outcomes, but a relationship is easy to intuit. Children with limited access are more likely to have routine and preventable illnesses, causing more frequent absences from school.

5. **Exposure to and absorption of lead in the blood:** Children with high blood lead levels are disproportionately from low-income families. Lead reduces cognitive ability (IQ) and causes adverse behavioral outcomes, such as increased violence and other criminal behavior in adolescents and young adults. Although lead was removed from gasoline in the 1970s and 1980s, lead remains on the ground and is frequently stirred up into breathable air. Lead also remains in windows, window frames, the walls of older buildings, and pipes carrying water to residences.[3]

Making Sense of the Data: How can parents overcome these barriers?

There are no easy answers to the cycle of poverty and low academic performance, but with maximum parental commitment and support, some of these barriers can be overcome.

I believe that changing a mother's attitude from that of an acceptance of failure to a can-do attitude of success is the critical variable that determines a child's success or failure.

How do I know this, you ask? Because I see families without advantages who manage to do it all the time. Unfortunately, not all children being raised in poverty or near poverty are going to see the success that Devon managed to achieve. Devon was lucky—he got a great mom who was able to maintain a positive attitude toward her child's future and committed herself to that goal throughout his childhood.

The bigger challenge we have as a society is to figure out a way to transform every mom into a Devon mom. For readers who want to delve into this subject more in-depth, I strongly encourage you to read an excellent book by author Paul Tough entitled *Whatever it Takes*.

The Link Between Parental Commitment and Childhood Success

Why do students of Asian background, whether raised in Asia or elsewhere, on average, have higher performance in school—especially with respect to their math skills? Do these children have a genetic talent for mathematics, or could this have something to do with parenting and parental commitment as well?

After you look at the same statistics that I have, you will see that their aptitude is more learned than inherited. In her fascinating book entitled *Growing Up the Chinese Way*, Sing Lau makes a strong argument that there is something in the Chinese family's attitude toward academics—and possibly parenting in general—that leads Chinese children toward academic excellence.[4] The information that I am going to present in this section comes partly from Sing Lau's analysis.

Scientific studies confirm that most children, regardless of their heritage, are born with very similar native intelligence. We have all seen the famous bell curve, the graph that defines the spread of normal. This curve can define any characteristic that humans possess—from our speed of running a mile, the number of hairs on our heads, to even our memories or abilities to manipulate numbers.

Most children cluster near the average (also known as mean) with a pretty even spread above and below the mean. Some children are fortunate to have much better memories than average, but keep in mind that *most* are clustered very near the average. That is true across cultures as well. There is very little difference in the average aptitude (measure of academic performance) between Chinese children, Japanese children, and American children (children living in Minneapolis).[4]

I am struck with how similar the cognitive skills of all of these children were in this study. In both the first and fifth grades, data collected on the same children showed there is very little difference in their performance across a broad array of cognitive tests. These skills included serial memory for words, vocabulary, auditory memory, general information, verbal-spatial ability, verbal memory, coding, spatial relations, serial memory of numbers, and perceptual speed.

Now, let's look at what happens to children educated in these locations as they progress through their academic careers from the PISA data (Performance of International Schools Assessment), given to students around the world when they are fifteen years old.[5]

Despite the fact that American schools spend far more per pupil on education, and that the American and Asian children have essentially the same IQ and achievement when they enter school, the Asian students have taken the top spots as far as academic achievement across the board.

And the Asian students aren't scoring just a little better; they are *markedly* better at academics across all the fields-of-study tested. Being Asian is like being from radio host Garrison Keillor's fictitious Lake Wobegon, where all the women are strong, all the men are good-looking, and all the children are above average!

Ranking of Student Academic Achievement by Country-2012

Rank	OECD Average Score	Mean score in PISA Exam 494
1	Shanghai China	613
2	Singapore	573
3	Hong-Kong-China	561
4	Chinese Taipei	560
5	Korea	554
6	Macao-China	538
7	Japan	536
8	Liechtenstein	535

9	Switzerland	531
10	Netherlands	523
26	United Kingdom	494
36	United States	481
37	Sweden	478
44	Turkey	448
53	Mexico	413
58	Brazil	391
65	Peru	368

But what's up? How can this be that Asian children rise to the top so easily? Is something dramatic happening to the Asian children that is *not happening* to their American and other worldly counterparts? Experts think they know what the difference is—high *parental expectations* and *commitment* in their children's academic lives.

Picture this scene: After a family meal and cleanup has occurred, the dinner table is cleared off and all of the children and parents then collectively begin the evening's academic work, together, for however long it takes, for a child's entire primary educational years!

Parents help the older children when they need it, and older children help younger ones. Everyone is involved without the distractions of TV or socializing with friends on the phone. The family is totally focused on their children's academic success, and this focus takes priority over everything else.

This scene is very common in many Asian homes. I doubt that there are many homes from other cultures, which, as a family, invest this much energy into homework and school preparation. Take a look at this survey done by the Brookings Institute[6] on a broad slice of American high school students between 2003-2013, and you will quickly see the secret to Asian academic success and where others are falling short.

The Asian children are doing at least twice the amount of homework as their classmates. Now things are beginning to become much clearer. While Asian students, or average, have no more aptitude than their classmates from other cultures, *they just work much much harder*. What did Edison say? Success is 1% inspiration and 99% perspiration. And he was right—as the Asian families are proving.

Cultural differences also come into play, specifically that of parental expectations. What is it about growing up the Asian/Chinese way that allows so many Asian children to excel—particularly in math—if it isn't native ability? According to Sing Lau, it is harder work, having very high standards for their children, and living in a culture that values education very highly.[4]

These are powerful forces that propel so many Asian students to perform at the highest levels. *Effort over aptitude* seems to be the Asian formula. Where does this attitude have its roots? With strong parental commitment to the cause of their children's success.

Why are Asian students so motivated compared to other children?

Now let's take a look at what strong parental commitment to education can achieve. Clearly, the Chinese are doing something right at motivating their children toward hard work and achievement. I argue that the big X-factor (the gorilla in the room, so to speak) is high *parental expectations* and a willingness on the part of Asian parents to *commit* to their children's academic success.

Think about the scene I painted for you a few paragraphs back, that of the entire family committing most evenings to the children's academics. The message is very clear for the Asian children in these families—study is important and failure is not an option. Not only is failure not an option, but excelling is a must. Average is not good enough for most Asian parents. I don't see any other way to interpret these statistics. A strong parental commitment, not intelligence, explains Asian children's high performance.

Cautions Concerning Heavy Parental Involvement in a Child's Academic Life

Strong parental commitment is undoubtedly an important propelling force for all children, but one can argue that any parenting style that imposes intense pressure for achievement can potentially have very negative psychological effects for a child. Recall our discussion of parenting styles from Chapter 3 where we discovered that the most effective parenting style is *authoritative* (demanding but warm) not *authoritarian* (demanding but not response to a child's feelings). There is a limit to how much pressure parents can impose on their children before they either rebel, become overwhelmed with resentment, or experience a profound sense of failure. Balancing high academic standards with realistic expectations given a child's innate talents can be a difficult thing for many parents.

Futhermore, even if the high academic standards are achieved by the child, it is possible that focusing so intently on academic work may diminish their creative, social, and expressive abilities. It is possible that parental pressure for academic excellence can be so high that parents fail to see other talents and interests that their children may have. In other words, there are other talents that can serve a child as well as, or possibly better than, top-notch academic performance. Overly pressuring parents may fail to see these aspects of their children's personalities. In my mind, the goal of all parents should be to maximize their children's potential and not to create class valedictorians.

Conclusion

Strong parental commitment to the success of children is a fundamental ingredient in the recipe for producing a Great Kid. It is the spark that ignites the engine. It is the wind in the sails of any child. I believe it is one of the foundations of parenting a Great Kid, and an ingredient that is fundamental to a child's long-term success. Recall the story of Devon and his mom.

You can now see the formula of producing a Great Kid becoming clearer: Provide appropriate rewards for your children's achievement, set high expectations for them, create a healthy emotional climate in which for them to grow up, invest a lot of your time and energy into your children's success, and you are well on your way to having yourself a Great Kid.

Add to that the authoritative parenting style we saw in Chapter 3, and you really have something going. You are well on your way to producing the kind of child every parent envies. With the addition of one more of the parenting foundations, you will understand the complete formula of raising a Great Kid.

Possible barriers to strong parental commitment.

As we saw earlier in this chapter, some families have far more hurdles to overcome than others to achieve the ideal amount of energy that can be invested into the children of the family. Here are a few barriers to consider, and if possible, try to remedy:

1. Many parents were given a poor example of how to raise children by their parents. These parents simply don't know how to be maximally supportive of their children.

2. Some parents do not spend enough energy and time to discover their children's talents and interests.

3. Many parents are overworked, spread too thin by long hours at work. Many have irregular, unpredictable work hours or have to work multiple jobs to meet the financial obligations of the family.

4. Some parents simply do not have the mental energy and good health to advocate for and propel their children.

5. Unfortunately, some children are raised with cultural messages that discourage their achievement.

6. Some families have an overemphasis on acquiring material things to the detriment of family time. This tendency can lead to parents making poor decisions with respect to allocation of time and money.

Now You Know

- Strong Parental Commitment is fundamental to a child's long-term success.

- Ingredients of Parental Commitment are:

    1. The promise of strong action on the child's behalf

    2. Hard work and time commitment on the part of the child's parent

    3. Unwavering loyalty to the child

    4. Publicly expressing an attitude of support toward the child

- Some of the barriers to a child's success are self-imposed limitations, which, with effort, are surmountable. Taking action to change these is essential.

- Evidence demonstrates that strong parental commitment is an important ingredient in producing Great Kids.

What Can You Do?

1. If you have friends who seem particularly good at supporting their children and parenting, emulate what they do or even ask them for help.

2. Try to identify your children's interests and talents and make sure to facilitate growth in these areas.

3. Provide as many cognitively stimulating activities as you can for your children, especially when they are young. Most importantly, read and talk to your children.

4. Many communities have organizations that help individuals find stable employment or possibly even career training classes. Try to find these opportunities if at all possible.

5. Recruit as many responsible, loving adults as you can— especially if your children are being raised in a single-parent household.

6. Make it a priority to get your children and yourself the best healthcare available.

7. Expect your children to be successful and communicate your expectations to them frequently. Your expectations of your children are far more important than any negative messages that your children may encounter in their community.

8. Always remember that your love, support, and participation in your children's lives is the most important legacy you can give them. Don't skimp.

6
Stability

"Families are like Slinkies®: stress any member and the whole family starts shaking."

Doc Smo *Pearl*
Portable Practical Pediatrics Podcast
December 28, 2011

The True Story of My Children's Elementary School:

Let's start our discussion of how important certainty and stability are to a child's well-being by looking at the school that my children attended. When my children were in elementary school, they attended a public school that drew students from two very different sections of town.

Because of this fact, student achievement differed greatly, in a "bimodal" fashion. In a bimodal school, some of the children achieve, on average, at a high academic level, and others reach, on average, a low mean level of academic success.

The name bimodal comes from the graph of their achievement. A bimodal school looks like two separate populations with two averages, rather than just one average (like most schools). Indeed, the school did have two populations of students attending. There were students from a neighborhood with mostly college-educated parents and students from a neighborhood with a disadvantaged population, mostly living in poverty.

All the children received their education in the same building, in the same classrooms, with the same teachers and books—and yet the skills learned (as measured by standardized tests) were very different. The school spent a tremendous amount of effort trying to equalize the performance of the two populations of students but were never able to adequately bridge the large gap.

The school had a psychologist who worked with children exhibiting behavior problems as well as academically low-achieving children. She, therefore, had tremendous insight into the lives of the struggling students. As part of her job, she frequently made home visits to the homes of many of these students. She functioned somewhat like a social worker in this respect. This psychologist spent a lot of time in the homes of very poor children and had a good feel for the struggles of these families.

During the years my children were at this school, I tutored some of the low-achieving students. This afforded me many opportunities to talk to the school psychologist about what she believed were the obstacles encountered by the low-achieving students.

She said it was obvious to her. The low-achieving students usually came from economically poor households that were headed by a single parent who often had little educational success themselves, who had difficulty supervising their children for a host of reasons, and who provided their children with limited exposure to sophisticated language, especially from books.

She told me that there were very few books in these homes and very little reading going on. She told me that many of these children only heard language such as "Sit down," "Stop that," or "Put that down."

She believed that the disadvantaged children possessed language skills far behind the advantaged children's. How could they keep up? Books and reading were not part of these family's routines. To make matters worse, these children didn't have a safe, stimulating, secure place to play and explore.

No, their single mothers were all too often at multiple jobs, struggling to make money and keep up with their bills and put food on the table for their families. Many were home with siblings in neighborhoods that were, frankly, dangerous.

You can see the pattern—an unstable, fragile family with few resources leading to a lack of security and slower learning. The lack of family stability (financial, housing, food, and caretaking), along with their lack of early opportunity for learning, and a lack of a secure environment to play and learn, put them at a major disadvantage at school. That disadvantage often persisted for the rest of their school careers. Some students overcame these impediments, but sadly, many did not.

Because of chronic failure, many of the disadvantaged children became angry by the time they had reached late elementary school. I think they realized that they were not likely to be able to keep up with many of the other children academically and simply got mad and gave up. They saw the obstacles as too large to overcome. Their anger eventually turned into behavior problems and a lack of effort or interest in school. They had given up—many by the 4th grade!

I believe the same children, had they had more stability in their family life, more resources, less stress, and more support, would have become far more successful students. I believe that family instability, in whatever form it may take, is at the root of many children's life difficulties. It is as simple as that.

A Pediatrician's Perspective

Children of various backgrounds, at the same age, look and act similar, even if their life experiences have been very different. So it was at my children's elementary school. Approximately 40% of the children who attended their school came from middle-class families. But the other 60% came from so-called "at-risk" or "disadvantaged" families, who were living in poverty when not at school.

Many had not had the advantages afforded to middle-class children: a home rich with books, parents who could provide steady food and shelter, and a parent who had successfully finished school.

The majority of the disadvantaged children at my children's school lived in single-parent households that experienced both food and housing insecurity.

Many of their single parents struggled with multiple low-paying jobs and were chronically exhausted. To make matters worse, a large proportion of these children's parents had not had much success in school themselves and were therefore ill-equipped to help their children succeed at school.

We know from the educational community that the skill levels of these two populations upon arrival at school were often very different. Listen to what experts at the Brookings Institute concluded in 2016 about the differences in school readiness between disadvantaged and advantaged children.

> Poor children start school at a disadvantage. Their health, behaviors, and skills make them less prepared for kindergarten than children growing up under better economic conditions. Fewer than half (48 percent) of poor children are school ready at age five, under a summary measure that encompasses early math and reading skills, learning-related and problem behaviors, and overall physical health. Children born to parents with moderate or higher incomes are much more likely to enter school ready to learn; three-fourths (75 percent) of these children are ready for school at age five. In other words, there is a 27 percentage point gap in school readiness between poor children and those from moderate or higher income families.[1]

Much of the difference at the time of school entry is due to what is called the "word gap." This term refers to the (often huge) difference between language skills of different children at the time of school entrance. Estimates are that a child from an advantaged household has heard approximately 30 million more words than their disadvantaged classmates. This is a staggering difference and one that contributes heavily to the bimodal achievement curve that my family witnessed at my children's elementary school.[2]

The instability that disadvantaged children experience in their day-to-day lives weighs heavily on them. I have experienced this first hand at my children's school and in my medical practice. Pediatricians know which families are struggling and which aren't.

Helping children and their families thrive in whatever environment in which they find themselves is one of the duties of a pediatrician.

Normal emotional growth is difficult for a child to achieve without a stable environment.

My thirty-seven years of practicing pediatrics has taught me that raising successful children (what I call Great Kids) is less about the children and more about the parents and the family environment that the parents create for their children.

Said another way, children live in the reality that their parents create for them. For me, that was an amazing revelation. As a pediatrician, I witness the tremendous positive or negative effect that a stable versus unstable family can have on a child.

When families function well, watching them mold their children into successful adults is one of the great joys of my job. But when there is instability and turmoil of any sort in a child's world, there is the potential for serious problems.

It is not unusual for me to care for a child with serious emotional, cognitive, or physical disabilities who, with a supportive, stable family in the background, achieves amazing success in school, employment, and life. Should the same child be born into a less stable family setting, one that has more stress and uncertainty in the family's daily life, my experience tells me that such a child is less likely to thrive and develop into a Great Kid.

I believe that changing a mother's attitude from that of an *acceptance of failure* to a *can-do attitude of success* is the critical variable that determines a child's success or failure.

Children live in the reality that
their parents create for them.

Doc Smo's definition of *family stability* versus *instability*

What do I mean by stability in a family? My definition of a *stable family* is one that provides unconditional love and support for a child, is able to consistently meet the child's basic needs, creates a predictable environment for the child, and one that doesn't present serious emotional uncertainty and distractions to a child's healthy personality development.

That's not to say that *any* change in a child's life (such as a family move, a job change by a parent, or a serious illness in a family member) will destroy the child's developmental path. No, every family encounters difficult times and needs to overcome life's ups and downs. But there is a level of instability that tips the scales away from a child's healthy development into the range of troublesome—especially when that instability is chronic.

I can't define exactly where that tipping point is, but I know it exists. I also know that a child who lives in a family with chronic or recurring instability is more likely to experience negative impacts. I've seen it play out many times. A child growing up with a high degree of life uncertainty begins to dwell on sadness, anxiety, anger, jealousy, or hopelessness.

At this level of instability, the child begins to veer away from normal psychological development and instead progresses along an alternate path. The level of instability required to cause this change varies according to the individual child, their age, their resiliency, and the intensity of the family instability.

Recall our discussion of Adverse Child Experience factors in Chapter 4? The more ACEs a child experiences, the more likely that child will experience serious physical and emotional consequences. How in the world can a child who is caught in an unstable family be expected to gain mastery over all the tasks Great Kids need to internalize?

What happens to children who experience instability during their childhoods?

Children have a tremendous amount to learn as they grow up. Family stress, uncertainty, and instability potentially slows, or even derails, age-appropriate personality development. Psychologists tell us that the critical tasks of childhood include the following:

- Learning to trust and love the child's primary caretaker (the basis of all of a child's future relationships)
- Learning to follow rules and social norms
- Mastering numerous life-skills
- Developing a healthy sense of uniqueness and self

- Learning how to relate and coexist with others in a healthy way

Failure to achieve any of these developmental tasks during childhood can interfere with normal healthy growth. One thing I have noticed in my practice with regards to family stress is that the younger the child is at the time of the stress, the stronger the impact the instability has on that child.

Additionally, I have noticed that children who endure serious uncertainty in their lives under the age of two years, or between the ages of four to six years, or between the ages of 11 to 13 years are more likely to experience ill effects as a consequence. These age ranges all seem to be critical time frames for personality development. They are particularly bad times to be stressed with uncertainty.

Consider for a moment that you are a child again and that your family presents you with one of the following situations:

1. You are bounced between various homes with various caretakers (each with a different set of rules and expectations).

2. You undergo frequent separation from your parent or parents for one reason or another.

3. You grow up in poverty.

4. Your family frequently experiences food and/or housing difficulties.

5. You witness physical or emotional violence around you.

6. You are aware of substance abuse within your home.

7. You are not able to establish long-term friendships because your family frequently moves.

I know that for myself, any of these situations would have had profound effects on my childhood and my personality.

Now imagine that your family presents you with *multiple destabilizing factors*—a combination of many of these circumstances. Some children posed with these life realities might cope well, but for me, I fear that I would have had serious emotional difficulties as a result.

The most common destabilizing factors
I see in my middle-class practice?

It is amazing to me how often I see very nice families have a difficult time providing a stable family life for their children. While many factors can disrupt family harmony, let me tell you about the things that I see most often.

Having a parent who suffers from a *mood disorder* such as anxiety or depression is all too frequent in America today. When I take family health histories, I am amazed at the percentage of parents who have mood difficulties and take anti-anxiety or antidepressant medications or have substance abuse problems. I think that the negative effects of having a parent with a mood disorder are very evident when viewed from the perspective of a pediatrician. These children often have sleep difficulties, multiple somatic complaints, as well as slow personality maturation.

Marital problems are also a common source of instability for children in my experience. I think we are all aware of the high failure rate of marriages today. Sadly, about 50% of marriages today end in separation and divorce. Many other marriages develop a toxic brew of hostility and parental strife that children in their households have to live in. I hear about this all the time from kids. Living with their parent's discord is a difficult situation for them. Whether it be complete divorce or its precursor, chronic long-term hostility between parents, this kind of family instability and uncertainty often colors their childhood in an extremely negative way.

And let's not forget *alcohol and other substance abuse* problems—a major league contributor to family instability and uncertainty. No discussion of unhealthy families can be complete without an analysis of the effect of alcohol and illegal drugs on parents. Alcohol dependence is amazingly common in our culture. In a recent survey done by the NIH revealed that 1 in 4 adults in the US binge drink.[3]

Frequent exposure to alcohol has deleterious effects on both body and soul. Heavy alcohol use can be harmful and deadly, but additionally, it can fracture a parent's ability to parent effectively. Along with alcohol dependency often comes erratic behavior, a tendency toward violence and extreme mood swings, difficulty maintaining healthy relationships with family members, and job and financial insecurity.

Chronic mood disorders among parents, marital disharmony, and alcohol and substance abuse are the problems I witness in the predominantly well-educated, middle-class families I care for. Keep in mind that more fragile "at-risk" populations have these problems *plus* the additional difficulties of chronic poverty, housing and food instability, and the disruption and dangers of living in an environment that may be inherently more dangerous.

"A Detour Down Science Drive"—Lack of Family Stability Causes Problems

While social science research is complicated, many studies show that family structure and the number of family transitions a child experiences correlate negatively with that child's ultimate success.

In other words, the more instability in a family (divorce, single-parent households, blended families, and cohabitation without marriage, etc.), the more likely the children raised in that household will have one of the markers of poor outcome. These markers are behavior difficulties, substance abuse, low cognitive ability, school failure, early initiation of sexual activity, and a lower age at the time of the birth of their first child.

While these are only statistical associations and don't *prove* that family instability *causes* negative childhood outcomes, this just makes sense and fits with most of our day-to-day experience. Sociologists have a name for this theory. They call it the "Instability Hypothesis."

Sociologists Fomby and Cherlin at Johns Hopkins studied the effect of family instability in a retrospective analysis of the data contained in the National Longitudinal Survey of Youth (NLSY79) and its 2000 mother-child supplement, the Children of the NLSY (CNLSY).[4] As you can see, the data they used involved a 21-year follow-up to measure outcomes. Such a long follow-up period is unusual in social science research and provided a valuable glimpse of the long-term associations with unstable households.

Their conclusion? Children of all races that were raised in single-mother families in their first four years had a much higher chance of serious behavioral difficulties during their life. As for a correlation between difficulties and the number of family *transitions* (divorce, remarriage, cohabitation, etc.), a negative effect was only seen among white children.

Take note of the fact that the negative impact of single parenting was particularly damaging to *very young* children. Psychologists have noted this for a long time, and again, this passes what I call the common sense rule. **Children are most vulnerable to trauma when they are very young or when they are changing rapidly.** There seem to be critical times in a child's development when instability has an added negative impact on a child. One of those periods is birth to five years of age.

Another large pool of data examining family instability and childhood outcomes has been collected by the Fragile Families and Child Wellbeing Study (FFCWS), a consortium of researchers at Princeton and Columbia Universities. These researchers have been collecting longitudinal data on cohorts of families and children since 1998.

Their conclusions are clear; family instability has negative effects on the children in these families. Here is a quote from the researchers analyzing the FFCWS data.

> The FFCWS studies add to a large body of earlier work that suggested that children who live with single or cohabiting parents fare worse as adolescents and young adults in terms of their educational outcomes, risk of teen birth, and attachment to school and the labor market than do children who grow up in married-couple families.[5]

Finally, let's look at children who grow up in military families where moves are frequent, social connections tend to be transient, and the stress of having a deployed family member getting injured (or even killed) is a reality that these children live with.

Here, evidence definitely documents and supports the negative effects of the instability that having a family member deployed in the military creates. Research done in 2010 found a strong correlation between having a parent deployed in the military and an increase in a child's chance of needing assistance with either a mental health or a behavior problem.[6]

Additionally, the AAP cited research in their 2013 statement about children in military families. According to their sources, the stress that military life puts on children is different at different ages. Here is their summary by age[7]:

Stress of Military Life on Children by Age

Feelings	Behaviors
Preschool • Confusion • Anger • Guilt	• Clinging, demands attention • Problems separating from the remaining parent • Irritability and aggression • Sleep disturbances • Feeding issues (more picky) • Easy frustration and more difficult to comfort
School age • Same feelings as preschool plus: • Increased sadness (lack of family normalcy and loss of deployed parent) • Worry about deployed parent • Fear that remaining parent might leave or die • Anger at parent for missing important events	• New behavior problems or intensification of already existing problems • Regression • Rapid mood swings • Changes in eating and sleeping • Anger at both parents for disrupting normalcy • Changes in behavior at school and with friends (anger, aggression) • Need to be and do "normal" things (eg parties) • Somatic complaints
Adolescent • Anger • Sadness • Depression • Anxiety • Fear	• Misdirected or acting out behavior toward others or themselves • School problems • Apathy, loss of interest, non-communication, and denial of feelings • Increased importance of friends to the detriment of reasonable family life • Trying to take charge of the family

Siegel, B. S., and Davis, B. E. "Health and Mental Health Needs of Children in US Military Families." *Pediatrics* 131, no. 6 (2013).

All of the research that I have presented points out how a lack of stability and predictability in a child's life negatively impacts their mental health and (possibly) ultimately, their wellbeing in life. It is fair to say that current research strongly suggests that parents should do everything they can to provide predictability, stability, and an environment of low stress for their children, especially when they are under five years of age.

> *Children are most vulnerable to trauma when they are very young or when they are changing rapidly.*

Why do children raised in stable families have more success?

I think you can now see that children raised in unstable families have a more difficult time achieving normal development. But why is this so? What is there about living in an unstable family that so often gets children in these households off track? While there are no simple answers, and every family has unique dynamics and stresses, I think the answer comes down to three main obstacles.

Reason #1—A less secure environment impairs cognitive development and healthy personality development.

Childhood is a time of learning and exploration. Think about what play is all about—constant exploration, testing assumptions about the world, pushing oneself physically, role-playing, and learning new things. Children have an insatiable appetite for learning and exploring. They never seem to tire of discovering new things.

This exploration can only occur, however, if they have a safe place in which to explore. Having a predictably safe place to explore the world is *fundamental* to exploration and learning. If a child is unsure of a parent's rules, fears a parent's negative emotional response to their actions, or is grieving the loss of a parent or sibling, learning is slowed. Play may even become associated with anxiety in a child.

I think it is safe to say that the less play and exploration a child experiences, the slower their cognitive development is likely to be. This may be the way instability in families negatively impacts their children's development.

Reason #2-Family stability allows a child to put their energy toward mastery of skills.

Children have to master an amazing number of skills in order to become independent adults. Every day is full of new knowledge. As anyone who has taken a foreign language understands, learning a new language, with its gigantic vocabulary, complex grammatical rules, and seemingly endless idioms, is a daunting task for anyone.

At the same time that children are learning an entirely new language, they are also learning many other things. Here are just a few:

- the rules of the house
- colors, shapes, numbers and letters
- how to read
- the norms of social interaction
- self help skills
- the joys and disappointments of friendships
- the concept of right and wrong
- their unique identity
- how to empathize
- how and when to stand up for oneself
- how to push their cognitive abilities to their limit

When all these tasks are taken on in a stable home with lots of love, support, and stability, most children are successful even though the list of things they must learn seems quite formidable.

Now let's consider what a child in an unstable family faces. Emotional turmoil diverts a child's energy away from learning new skills and directs it toward trying to learn to cope with whatever environmental stressor they are presented.

Imagine that you were trying to learn a new language or higher order math concepts and, at the same time, were upset, tired, or emotionally stressed. Your heightened emotional state would certainly impair your ability to both concentrate and learn.

This is what happens to children who have unstable families. They are often thrust into new living conditions, having secure relationships disrupted, or grieving the loss of one thing or another. I don't know about you, but I would not be able to learn very effectively under these circumstances.

Reason #3—A safe, accepting environment gives a child a chance to learn to recognize and manage their own temperament and limitations.

An important determinant of a child's ultimate personality is their innate temperament. Any parent who has had multiple children realizes that despite very similar treatment, their children seem to have their own natural personalities and ways of reacting to the world. Psychologists call these traits "temperament."

Temperament is thought to be a biologically determined set of traits that is pre-set from the time of birth. Up until the mid-twentieth century, babies were considered to be "blank slates" at birth with parenting being the only influence that affected a baby's personality.

Things changed when two American psychiatrists, a husband and wife team of researchers, Alexander Thomas M.D. and Stella Chess M.D, began studying and categorizing temperament in children. Their work started back in the 1950s with a longitudinal study of infant and child temperament they termed the "New York Study." Their study group consisted of 238 white and Hispanic children living in New York.[8]

After decades of research, they concluded that there are four main types of child temperaments—*easy or flexible, difficult, slow to warm or cautious, and mixed*.[9] The frequencies of each of the subtypes of temperament among children are estimated to be roughly[10]:

New York Longitudinal Study
Estimate of Temperament Frequencies

- Easy-40%
- Difficult-10%
- Slow to Warm-15%
- Mixed 35%

Since Thomas and Chess discovered that not all babies are born with the same temperament, many variations and refinements have been added to their original classification system by other psychologists. It is now generally agreed that a child's temperament, along with the type of parenting he or she receives, is an important determinant of their ultimate personality.

Now consider how children with these different temperament types fare in various kinds of families. For our purposes, we are going to think of families as either stable or unstable for simplicity. An *easy or flexible* child will probably not be *as* affected by being born into an unstable family as one that is either *difficult* or *slow to warm or cautious*.

Stable families have more resources at their disposal, are better able to cope with a difficult child, and are much more likely to provide what difficult temperament children need Stable families have the resiliency and flexibility to allow a difficult temperament child to learn to cope with their own temperament.[11]

The same is true for children with physical or emotional disabilities—stable families allow the child to learn to cope with their disability. I see this all the time. As a pediatrician, I recognize these resilient families very quickly and love to see these children overcome whatever disability they have.

Now You Know

- Family stability is one of the essential ingredients children need for healthy emotional development—to achieve Great Kid status.

- Stable families are supportive, predictable, loving, and are able to promote and nurture positive qualities in their children.

- The evidence is strong that the more transitions a child endures during childhood, the more difficulty the child has in obtaining physical and emotional health, especially when the child is very young.

- Children raised in unstable households lack the secure environment they need to maximize their cognitive and emotional development.

- Children raised in unstable environments have more difficulty learning to manage their own temperament.

- Families that provide stability for their children are able to help their children overcome huge obstacles during childhood.

What Can You Do?

1. Create as much routine and sameness in children's lives as possible. Predictability is the opposite of instability.

2. Utilize all resources available. Lean on family and friends. Recruit help from church, school, and even neighbors. I think when you begin asking for assistance, you will be surprised at the resources at your disposal.

3. If you are experiencing housing or food instability, consider having your family live with a relative or in a more stable household.

4. If you have a child with a difficult temperament, seek professional help. See how professionals can help manage the situation without you needing to resort to overly forceful means.

5. Avoid change during particularly "vulnerable periods of child development" if possible. These periods are: under two years of age, between three and five years of age, and 11-13 years.

6. Whenever possible, put the needs of your children first

7. Always remember that children seek a parent's *attention*, *love*, and *protection* above everything else. Material things are nice but not nearly as important to a child as your love and approval. To the best of your ability, provide these ingredients.

8. If you are a parent with a drinking problem or emotional illness, seek help. These problems can be overcome.

9. If you find yourself in an abusive situation, take immediate action to improve things for your family. Most towns have women's shelters and other social service supports—but you need to ask for help.

10. If your family has any ACE factors (refer to Chapter 3 for the full list) that you can eliminate, do so.

11. In all aspects of your life, put aside your desire for material things in favor of stability when you have children in the house to raise.

7

The Great Kid Recipe

*"There are no do-overs when it comes to childhood; this is the only childhood that your children will ever have.
Make the most of it!"*

Doc Smo *Pearl*
Portable Practical Pediatrics Podcast
December 2, 2018

The factors that determine the personality of a child are undoubtedly complex and multifactorial—a mixture of genetics, environment, and life circumstance. Despite this, there are predictable, mutable factors that are of paramount importance as a child develops.

The good news is that parents have a large degree of control over the factors that shape their children's personality, tenacity, resiliency, and life goals. Helping parents find the conditions that will optimize the growth and development of their children—*your* children—is the reason that I penned this book. **As the title says, Great Kids Don't Just Happen.** Rather, I contend, they are molded, shaped, and *produced*.

I firmly believe that if parents get the five pillars of parenting we have discussed in the previous chapters *mostly* right, it is hard for them not to raise a Great Kid. Inversely, when any of these factors are missing, it is very easy for the child or children to be derailed from normal psychological development and end up where no one wants them to be.

We have seen the devastating effects that family instability, poverty, and emotional or physical violence can impose on a young child in our discussion of the ACE factors. I hope you now see the same dangers when parents are poor at using praise, are ambivalent about limit-setting for their children, immerse their children in an unhealthy emotional family environment, aren't fully committed to their children, and fail to provide stability for them.

Parents have to make every effort to get their parenting house in order, to the best of their abilities. Recall from that discussion, many of the scars the ACE factors cause don't appear for decades into that child's life. When it comes to childhoods, unfortunately, there are no do-overs. This is the only childhood that your child will ever have, and it is you, their parents, that create the reality in which your child lives. You need to create the healthiest environment you know how to, and help your child make the most of their opportunities.

Fortunately, parenting doesn't need to be perfect for children to thrive. My experience has shown me, however, that the closer a family can come to providing the parenting basics we have discussed, the more likely their child will reach Great Kid status.

I dare say that every family has stress, weaknesses, and flaws. It is precisely because of this fact that parents need to know and recognize when their family is moving away from the ideal and make every attempt to provide the forces I have described in the preceding chapters: effective use of praise and limit setting, a healthy emotional environment, strong parental commitment, and as much stability as possible.

You don't need to be flawless humans or perfect parents. But what I have observed is that parents who find the right balance of these developmental ingredients seem to produce the most successful children, using the definition of success that we previously discussed. Thirty-seven years of watching families grapple with family life tell me that these principles are important.

The good news is that parents have a large degree of control over the factors that shape their children's personality, tenacity, resiliency, and life goals.

While all of the pillars of parenting are important at every stage of a child's development, some play a more important role at different ages. Infants, toddlers, and preschool children are most in need of security and a safe, predictable environment in which to learn and explore. Children this age are keenly aware of their need for protection. It's their parents that provide that secure attachment.

Think about an older infant or toddler's reaction to being separated from their parents—shrieking and chaos! Or how about a preschooler's reaction to an accidental scrape or fall—hysteria with the immediate need for reassurance that they will be "okay". Fear of abandonment and fear of bodily damage are just under the surface of the life of a young child. Helping them through this worry is the foundation of a happy life as we saw in Chapter 4.

Consequently, having a stable, safe environment with parents who have a strong commitment to their well being are the most critical developmental essentials for children of this age range. The lesson the child learns when parents come to the rescue? Things happen, but my parents are always there to help. Everything will work out.

The school-age years are full of learning, skill development, and a growing need to please the adults in their life: parents, teachers, and others. The child is beginning to measure their behavior and skills against that of their peers and the expectations of teachers and other adults.

Mastering skills and pleasing the adults in a child's life are usually the prime motivators for school-age children. Think about what happens when school-aged children experience the disapproval of parents and teachers. Many reflexly lie and try and cover up the reason for their parent's disapproval. They likely know that lying is wrong but fear their parents' disapproval so much that they are willing to take the risk of being caught in a lie to avoid admitting their failures.

This is why the skillful and consistent use of praise and consequences is so essential during this period in a child's life. Appropriate use of praise and consequences is essential for the healthy emotional development of children in this age group.

Finally, the turmoil of the teen years come. Anyone who has raised a teenager knows that testing limits, resisting parental wishes, exploring for a unique identity, needing acceptance by peers, gaining more responsibilities, and beginning life goals seem to define most teens. Here is where firm limit-setting is the parental skill most needed.

Could this be why children raised in families without fathers tend to have more risk-taking behavior among their children? I think it goes without saying that fathers are in a unique role to enforce limits for their children. Their parental authority can be very strong. In my opinion, the teen years, with all the tension between parents and their children, is the age most in need of having consistent limit-setting for children.

My thirty-seven years in pediatrics has convinced me of one thing; if parents provide a good parenting foundation, it is very difficult for them not to have successful children. As we saw in a few of my family vignettes, families that have additional handicaps such as poverty, a single-parent household, or a physical or learning disability in their children, still seem to achieve success if the pillars of parenting are provided for their children. I see this played out over and over in my interactions with children and parents. I have confidence that great parenting creates resilient children that can overcome many of life's unfortunate circumstances.

One Final Story, That of WT

One final story I want to share with you: that of WT, a child with a form of autism called Asperger's Syndrome. I first met WT when his mother brought him for his yearly checkup. At the time, he was on summer break from school. After our introductions, his mother handed me a note she had prepared to fill me in on some of WT's health and developmental issues. With her permission, I am going to share her note with you with some minor changes to protect his identity and privacy:

Dear Dr. Smolen,

WT really liked his previous female pediatrician, but he is so pleased to have a male physician now that he is getting older! If you look through his chart notes, you can tell he has been through a lot-starting with a diagnosis of Pervasive Developmental Disability-Not Otherwise Specified from developmental pediatrics at a major children's hospital. He is a nice young man and generally a joy to have around the house—although he can be easily irritated and somewhat inflexible in some circumstances. But, this year has been difficult for him, and adolescence has hit him pretty hard.

I have written a little more about him below, so you can get to know him a little better and know what his current interests and concerns are:

Under care of:

- Many pediatric specialists

Current medications:

- ADHD medication
- Antipsychotic medication (being tapered in order to discontinue)
- Antidepressant

WT just graduated from his current grade. He had a rocky year this year and is grateful the school year has ended. His previous school years had been really good years for him. He was generally upbeat and felt like he had someplace to fit at school through participating in a few school activities, but this year it seems like the wheels fell off a bit and things got more difficult-both socially and academical y.

He had an increase in [OCD-obsessive compulsive symptoms] this year as well as an increase in tics—the most prevalent of those being throat clearing. He frequently felt depressed, unmotivated and misunderstood. Some of the kids at school were tough on him, but he is not completely without friends and does have a group of boys he relates to and hangs out with some. Trying to figure out medications for him this year has been difficult, and once we hit on something that seemed to help, his HgA1C was affected to the point that we are trying to discontinue the medication possibly responsible. He is very glad the school year is over and is looking forward to starting at a new school next fall.

WT likes playing video games, making videos, [and playing various sports]. He enjoys fishing, camping and traveling and is looking forward to doing all of those things this summer. He is not averse to trying new things and generally has a pretty affectionate nature. He is a very good at many of the activities he pursues. However, this year, he chose not to participate in some activities, citing his problems with OCD and tics.

I would appreciate it if you had a conversation about how much "screen time" is appropriate—particularly during the summer when he has more freedom. If it were allowed, he would probably spend all day doing something online. Recently, he expressed that his time online helped him relax and feel better about social interactions—which we understand, to some extent. We do monitor the sites he visits and they seem pretty benign at this point. We are trying to find some other things he is interested in to occupy his time and any suggestions you have would be appreciated. We will travel a lot this summer, but we will also try to get him to try some music lessons and do some volunteer work through church and possibly other organizations. Also, we will make sure he gets some exercise.

Thank You!

DT (Mom)

I think it is easy to see that WT is thriving, largely as a consequence of his family. I have just given you some excerpts from the note that WT's mother wrote to me that day. The note easily took an hour or two to prepare. This fact in itself shows a level of *parental commitment* that I don't often see. You can feel the *stability* and structure that W's family provides for him. They have managed to allow him freedom but at the same time create enough structure (*limits*) in his life to ensure that his maturity and acquisition of life skills can continue to develop.

I also sensed from this note that WT is immersed in a very healthy emotional environment. The implicit message throughout this mom's note is one of optimism and a positive view of her son and his future. Remember, we are talking about a child with a severe developmental disability—a form of autism.

For any parent to maintain optimism when faced with the reality of childhood autism requires a lot of personal strength and love. I am certain that WT has presented his family with many challenges and frustrating moments throughout his childhood. Maybe they even felt overwhelmed at times. Those feelings didn't matter to WT's mother. She stayed focused like a laser beam on making his future all that it could be. And look at what she was able to help him achieve! When she looks at WT, she doesn't see disability; she sees potential. To me, that is the definition of a *healthy emotional environment*.

While this note does not specifically address *praise*, I certainly would expect this mom not to be heaping undeserved praise on WT. As for consequences, I definitely got the sense that he experiences consequences when his behavior is out of bounds. Finally, when it comes to *limit setting*, I think it is obvious that this mom has no issues there. Consider her comments about limiting WT's screen time, making sure he doesn't wander into dangerous places on the internet, and filling his spare time with positive activities like volunteer work and travel.

Even though WT has very significant emotional and developmental disabilities and challenges, he is overcoming each and every barrier with the help of his family. He is getting a good education tailored to his needs. He is making social connections despite having a disability known for experiencing difficulty in this realm. He is even becoming involved in a positive way with his community through volunteer work and learning essential life skills he will need as an adult. All of this is happening because his family is providing exactly what he needs.

When I read this note his mother brought to me at his checkup, I could feel the energy and investment his family has made in him. I am sure he can feel it as well. They surrounded him with stability, gave him a healthy emotional environment, committed themselves to providing a strong parental presence, created appropriate expectations and praise, as well as formulated age and disability appropriate limits for him.

They got it all right, and WT is the beneficiary. He is thriving while many others in similar circumstances are not. The combination of the five factors we have discussed has molded WT into a wonderful success story. When I met him and his family, I thought, "What a lucky guy!"

Time for Some Self-Assessment

Now, let's take what we have seen in the preceding chapters and start to focus this knowledge on *your* family. If you are a parent of children of any age, take some time to assess whether you are providing the optimal environment for your children with respect to the five parenting pillars we have discussed in the preceding chapters. See if there are aspects of your parenting that need some improvement.

Be honest with yourself. You are not getting a grade, but rather you are making sure you are giving your child the best opportunity to become a Great Kid that you can. Use the foundations we have explored as your lens through which to view your family. I want you to make an honest assessment of what you are providing your children. Let's look at them one at a time:

Realistic praise:

It's my opinion that the self-esteem movement of psychologists and schools during the 1980s set effective parenting back a long way. It is one thing to pay close attention to identifying your child's talents and praising their achievements, but it is unhealthy to blindly praise their every action in hopes of raising their self-esteem.

Parents often feel that this is the right approach in this day, but evidence shows the contrary as we have previously discussed in Chapter 2. I think it is safe to say that many of today's parents have great difficulty not overpraising their children.

Every parent needs to periodically do a strong and honest self-assessment concerning their use of praise and make adjustments accordingly. Giving your child realistic feedback about their strengths and weaknesses, within the safety and privacy of their family, is essential for a child's healthy development—and a task that parents need to provide.

Similarly, I think today's parents are having great difficulty in allowing their children to experience the negative consequences of their behavior. No one likes to see their child fail, but failure is the spark that drives children toward success. A life without failure is unnatural and, in my view, very unhealthy.

In sports, children need to learn to be gracious losers as well as gracious winners. When children fail at an academic endeavor, that failure motivates them to try harder the next time. When they hurt another child's feelings or do them harm in another way, they need to learn how to rectify things without the help of parental intervention. Only with the tension between praise and consequences can they learn to balance their interactions with the demanding world they face today and in the future.

Consistent limits:

Ask any parent who has a child who attends daycare, and they will most likely tell you that the transition time between leaving the daycare and re-entering their own homes is one of the most difficult times for toddlers and young children. The transition between caretakers and settings, each with their own set of rules and expectations, is very difficult. There isn't consistency in the rules between the two settings.

Similarly, observe what happens when a classroom of elementary students experiences a change in teachers. The new teacher is not as predictable to the students as the one they had come to know, and rules and norms that had been enforced consistently up until that point in the school year all change. The behavior of the students is likely to suffer for a while during the transition.

When it comes to parenting teenagers, consistency is of the utmost importance. Think about families you have known where one parent is more permissive about enforcing rules than the other. The child sees their parent's inconsistency as an opportunity to test boundaries and potentially become outright defiant. Children of all ages like to have consistent limits. Rules that are consistent make a child's world more predictable and manageable.

I hope I have convinced you that creating clear boundaries for your children is vital to good parenting. Now it is time to see if you are good at limit-setting for your children. Ask yourself these things: Is my limit-setting predictable and consistent? Am I clear in the way I tell my children what I expect of them? Do I overreact in emotional ways when I try and enforce limits for my children? Or worst of all, do I belittle my children when they fail to meet my expectations?

Not sure how you are doing? Just ask your children, if they are old enough. This could be a very informative family meeting. If you feel that you are missing the mark on limit-setting, relax. This is one of the easiest pillars of parenting to rectify. Just make up your mind to do it!

Healthy emotional environment:

Now I want you to consider the *emotional temperature* of the household you have created for your children. Are your family member's emotions pretty even most of the time or are there frequent explosions, especially among the adults in the household? Are there any serious emotional problems among the adults in the household like depression, alcohol or drug dependency, or frequent threats of violence?

What I observed and provided you with evidence of, is that when families expose their child to an excess amount of anger, worry, sadness, or guilt, the children suffer. The energy the child would normally put toward healthy growth and development is instead channeled toward coping with their family's unhealthy emotional environment.

A child should not be consumed with worry about their parents breaking up or whether the child is the cause of their parent's drinking problems. I see these unfortunate circumstances all the time.

And remember that exposure to an unhealthy emotional environment has a bigger impact when it is thrust on infants, early school-aged children, and young teens. Children seem to be particularly vulnerable to unhealthy emotional environments at these ages.

If your young children are living in this kind of household, do everything you can to change that situation. There are things you can do that will help. It is vital for your children's future that you do so. Confronting these problems is likely to be uncomfortable, but you owe it to your children to make every effort to do so. Just your recognition of your child's difficult situation and empathy for your child may go a long way towards helping them cope.

Strong parental commitment:

Next, it is time to consider where your parenting falls on the involvement scale. It is important for you to understand that there is a difference between parents being strongly committed to their children's well-being versus taking over too much control of their children's lives. This situation can be detrimental to a child's independence and motivation. Many parents confuse these two types of involvement.

You can clearly see the distinction between parental involvement and commitment through the following examples of overly-involved parents. These are common patterns of parental behavior that I believe may signal overinvolvement:

- Parents who spend large amounts of money and time training their children to excel in a particular extracurricular activity, to the exclusion of other activities.

- Parents who make a habit of intervening in their school-aged and older children's conflicts with other children.

- Parents who accept that their children are always right. These parents often have difficulty seeing their own children's faults.

- Parents who will do almost anything to shield their children from failures and distress.

- Parents who make a habit of siding with their children when they come into conflict with adults.

- Parents who are so invested in their children's success that they fail to have their own interests and pursuits.

- Do any of those traits sound like your parenting? If so, take some time to consider your role in your children's lives and whether it is healthy. It has been my experience that children who have parents who frequently interact with them as I just described *do not* end up as resilient as children whose parents take a more hands-off approach to their parenting.

I think this is true because the overly involved or controlling parents place too much emphasis on protecting their child from discomfort and don't allow them to learn from the consequences of their actions. There is a difference between parental *over-involvement* in a child's life and parents who provide *strong parental commitment* for their children. The difference, at first glance, seems nuanced. But take into account the features of strongly committed parents:

- Parents who are emotionally accessible to their children.

- Parents who help their children make sense of their emotions and experiences.

- Parents who put their children's wellbeing in front of their own.

- Parents who are able to share both the joy of their children's successes and the sorrows of their failures.

- Parents who are always advocates for their children's well-being without being overly protective.

- Here is where I want your parenting to end up. These parenting traits promote healthy development among children. Commit them to memory and live them with your children.

Stability:

Finally, I want you to realistically assess the amount of stability (or lack of stability) your children are being exposed to. Consider how often your children are confronted with experiences that create uncertainty in their lives. Remember, uncertainty is the opposite of stability. I realize that this assessment may be difficult for you because it may involve admitting some of your shortcomings—never an easy thing to do.

Let's be careful not to confuse disappointment and failures in a child's life with instability in their family. Everyone is going to have disappointments and failures in their life. These are often some of the best learning experiences a child can have. Overcoming failure is what molds and defines a successful person. Failure is the fuel that propels a child to double down, put in more effort, and ultimately become successful at whatever is their goal.

This is not what I am talking about with regards to instability. I think of instability as a life circumstance that diverts a child's energy from moving forward in their developmental process that we call childhood. Here are some common forms of instability children encounter:

- Parents who can't get along
- Situations where children are forced to worry about their parents arguing or even divorcing
- Having to move frequently from school to school
- Food and housing uncertainty
- Parental job insecurity
- Not being given opportunities to develop meaningful friendships
- Having one or more parents with untreated mental health problems
- Having one or more parents with a substance abuse problem
- Having parents who are socially isolated and without much emotional support from family and friends
- These are big problems, you say, and very difficult to control. Yes, but many of these situations are amenable to change by proactive parents. Many involve simply asking

for help. If you recognize any of these situations, run, walk, or crawl and get some help. Your children only get one childhood, and their future is at stake.

Time for Action

It is now time for you to sit down and make a realistic assessment of the family environment you have created for your children. Take the five parameters we have explored, one at a time, and assess how your family is doing. Are you doing as well as possible or are there changes you can make that might benefit your children?

Life deals most families unfortunate circumstances from time to time. This fact we cannot control, but we can try to react with positive actions. We owe our children the best childhood that we can possibly provide.

Maximizing the stability in your home, keeping the emotional environment healthy and positive, committing all the energy you can toward their welfare, using praise and consequences properly, and setting realistic, consistent limits for them improves your chances of raising a child who is confident, emotionally stable, balanced, and capable. As I always say, "Great Kids don't just happen; they are made."

Best wishes and best of luck,
Doc Smo

About the Author

Dr. Paul Smolen, also known as Doc Smo by his friends, is a graduate of Duke University (1974), Rutgers Medical School (1978), and Wake Forest University-N.C. Baptist Hospital (1982). At Wake Forest University he completed a residency in general pediatrics, served as chief resident, and completed a fellowship in ambulatory pediatrics. Subsequently, he became board certified by the American Board of Pediatrics in 1983 and completed his maintenance of certification through 2019.

For the last 37 years, he has been an Adjunct Associate Professor of Pediatrics at the University of North Carolina-Chapel Hill, helping to train a generation of medical students and pediatric residents as well as author numerous research papers. He is currently a practicing pediatrician in Charlotte, NC.

Doc Smo is a bona-fide expert in knowing what parents want and need to know about parenting and child health. He shares practical and useful advice with parents and children alike, firmly believing that "an informed parent is a great parent."

Whether teaching, practicing, blogging or writing, Doc Smo's mission is to improve the health and well-being of children.

Follow Doc Smo at:
www.docsmo.com

Endnotes

Chapter 1

[1] Livingston, Gretchen. (Dec. 2014). Fewer than half of U.S. kids today live in a 'traditional' family. *Pew Research Center.* Available at: https://www.pewresearch.org/fact-tank/2014/12/22/less-than-half-of-u-s-kids-today-live-in-a-traditional-family/. [Accessed 12 June 2019].

[2] Mollborn, Stefanie. (June 2011). Norms About Nonmarital Pregnancy and Willingness to Provide Resources to Unwed Parents. *National Center for Biotechnology Information.* Available at: https://www.ncbi.nlm.nih.gov/pmc/articles/PMC3117423/. [Accessed 12 June 2019].

[3] McPherson, Miller et al. (June 2006). Social Isolation in America: Changes in Core Discussion Networks over Two Decades. *SAGE journals.* Available at: https://journals.sagepub.com/doi/abs/10.1177/000312240607100301. [Accessed 12 June 2019].

[4] *Childtrends.* (2013). Percentage of Children Living Below Selected Poverty Thresholds: Selected Years, 1959-2014. Available at: https://www.childtrends.org/wp-content/uploads/2014/09/04_fig1.jpg. [Accessed 12 June 2019].

[5] *American Academy of Pediatrics.* (Dec. 2011). The Pediatrician's Role in Family Support and Family Support Programs. Available at: https://pediatrics.aappublications.org/content/128/6/e1680. [Accessed 12 June 2019].

Chapter 2

[1] Sax, Leonard. (Dec. 2015). *The Collapse of Parenting.* Basic Books.

[2] Munger, Dave. (Aug. 2007). Basic concepts: Reinforcement and punishment. *ScienceBlogs*. Available at: https://scienceblogs.com/cognitivedaily/2007/08/06/basic-concepts-reinforcement-a. [Accessed 12 June 2019].

[3] Belsky, J. Ph.D. (Sept. 2008). Rewards are Better than Punishment: Here's Why. *Psychology Today*. Available at: https://www.psychologytoday.com/us/blog/family-affair/200809/rewards-are-better-punishment-here-s-why. [Accessed 12 June 2019].

[4] Bronson, Po; Merryman, Ashley. (Aug. 2009). *NurtureShock: New Thinking About Children* (p. 14). Grand Central Publishing. Kindle Edition.

[5] Haimovitz, Kyla; Corpus, Jennifer. (April 2011). Effects of Person versus Process Praise on Motivation in Emerging Adulthood. *American Educational Research Association*. Available at: https://www.reed.edu/motivation/docs/Haimovitz_Corpus_AERA.pdf. [Accessed 12 June 2019].

[6] Henderlong, Jennifer; Lepper, Mark. (2002). The Effects of Praise on Children's Intrinsic Motivation: A Review and Synthesis. *Reed College*. Available at: https://www.reed.edu/motivation/docs/PraiseReview.pdf. [Accessed 12 June 2019].

[7] Green, Morris; Solnit, Albert; (July 1964). Reactions to the Threatened Loss of a Child: A Vulnerable Child Syndrome. *American Academy of Pediatrics*. Available at: https://pediatrics.aappublications.org/content/34/1/58. [Accessed 12 June 2019].

[8] Perrin, Ellen et al. (March 1989). Is My Child Normal Yet? Correlates of Vulnerability. *American Academy of Pediatrics*. Available at: https://pediatrics.aappublications.org/content/83/3/355.short. [Accessed 12 June 2019].

Chapter 3

[1] Baumrind, Diana. (1966). Effects of authoritative parental control on child behavior. *Child Development* 37(4): 887-907.

[2] Baumrind, Diana. (1991). The influence of parenting style on adolescent competence and substance use. *Journal of Early Adolescence* 11(1): 56-95.

[3] Rodgers, Fred. (n.d.). *Fred Rodgers Productions*. Available at: https://www.fredrogers.org/parents/everyday-experiences/everyday-limits.php. [Accessed 12 June 2019].

Chapter 4

[1] Silver, Katie. (June 2014). Romania's lost generation: inside the Iron Curtain's orphanages. *ABC Radio National*. Available at: https://www.abc.net.au/radionational/programs/allinthemind/inside-the-iron-curtain%E2%80%99s-orphanages/5543388. [Accessed 12 June 2019].

[2] Powell, Alvin. (Oct. 2010). Breathtakingly awful. *The Harvard Gazette*. Available at: http://news.harvard.edu/gazette/story/2010/10/breathtakingly-awful/. [Accessed 12 June 2019].

[3] Lupien, Sonja J et al. (April 2009). Effects of stress throughout the lifespan on the brain, behaviour and cognition. *Springer Nature: Nature Reviews Neuroscience*. Available at: http://www.nature.com/nrn/journal/v10/n6/abs/nrn2639.html. [Accessed 12 June 2019].

[4] Hodel, Amanda et al. (Oct. 2014). Duration of Early Adversity and Structural Brain Development in Post-Institutionalized Adolescents. *National Center for Biotechnology Information*. Available at: https://www.ncbi.nlm.nih.gov/pmc/articles/PMC4262668/. [Accessed 12 June 2019].

[5] *Centers for Disease Control and Prevention*. (n.d.). About the CDC-Kaiser ACE Study. Available at: https://www.cdc.gov/violenceprevention/childabuseandneglect/acestudy/about.html. [Accessed 12 June 2019].

[6] *National Council of Juvenile and Family Court Judges*. Adverse Childhood Experience (ACE) Questionnaire: Finding your ACE Score. Available at: http://www.ncjfcj.org/sites/default/files/Finding%20Your%20ACE%20Score.pdf. [Accessed 12 June 2019].

[7] Reavis, James A. Psy.D. et al. (Spring 2013). Adverse Childhood Experiences and Adult Criminality: How Long Must We Live before We Possess Our Own Lives?. *National Center for Biotechnology Information*. Available at: https://www.ncbi.nlm.nih.gov/pmc/articles/PMC3662280/. [Accessed 12 June 2019].

8 Franke, Hillary A. (Nov. 2014). Toxic Stress: Effects, Prevention and Treatment. *National Center for Biotechnology Information*. Available at: https://www.ncbi.nlm.nih.gov/pmc/articles/PMC4928741/. [Accessed 12 June 2019].

9 Powell, Alvin. (Feb. 2012). Decoding keys to a healthy life. *The Harvard Gazette*. Available at: https://news.harvard.edu/gazette/story/2012/02/decoding-keys-to-a-healthy-life/. [Accessed 12 June 2019].

10 Doward, Jamie. (Nov. 2014). Emotional health in childhood 'is the key to future happiness'. *The Guardian*. Available at: https://www.theguardian.com/society/2014/nov/08/happiness-childhood-emotional-health-richard-layard. [Accessed 12 June 2019].

11 Layard, Richard et al. (Nov. 2014). What Predicts a Successful Life? A Life-Course Model of Well-Being. *National Center for Biotechnology Information*. Available at: https://www.ncbi.nlm.nih.gov/pmc/articles/PMC4240315/#SD1. [Accessed 12 June 2019].

Chapter 5

1 *Merriam Webster Online*. (2019). Definition of Commitment. Available at: https://www.merriam-webster.com/dictionary/commitment. [Accessed 12 June 2019].

2 Dubow, Eric et al. (July 2009). Long-term Effects of Parents' Education on Children's Educational and Occupational Success: Mediation by Family Interactions, Child Aggression, and Teenage Aspirations. *National Center for Biotechnology Information*. Available at: https://www.ncbi.nlm.nih.gov/pmc/articles/PMC2853053/. [Accessed 12 June 2019].

3 Morsey, Leila and Rothstein, Richard. (June 2015). Five Social Disadvantages That Depress Student Performance: Why Schools Alone Can't Close Achievement Gaps. *Economic Policy Institute*. Available at: https://www.epi.org/publication/five-social-disadvantages-that-depress-student-performance-why-schools-alone-cant-close-achievement-gaps/. [Accessed 12 June 2019].

4 Sing, Lau. (April 1996). *Growing Up the Chinese Way: Chinese Child and Adolescent Development*. The Chinese University Press.

[5] *Performance of International Schools Assessment.* Snapshot of Performance in Mathematics, Reading, and Science. (2012). Available at: https://cdn.theatlantic.com/assets/media/img/posts/pisa-2012-results-overview%20graph%201_larger.jpg. [Accessed 12 June 2019].

[6] Hansen, Michael and Quintero, Diana. (Aug. 2017). Analyzing 'the homework gap' among high school students. *The Brookings Institution.* Available at: https://www.brookings.edu/blog/brown-center-chalkboard/2017/08/10/analyzing-the-homework-gap-among-high-school-students/. [Accessed 12 June 2019].

Chapter 6

[1] Isaacs, Julia B. (Mar. 2012). Starting School at a Disadvantage: The School Readiness of Poor Children. *The Brookings Institution.* Available at: https://www.brookings.edu/wp-content/uploads/2016/06/0319_school_disadvantage_isaacs.pdf. [Accessed 12 June 2019].

[2] Lahey, Jessica. (Oct. 2014). Poor Kids and the 'Word Gap': The White House launches a new literacy initiative aimed at low-income children. *The Atlantic.* Available at: https://www.theatlantic.com/education/archive/2014/10/american-kids-are-starving-for-words/381552/. [Accessed 12 June 2019].

[3] *National Institute on Alcohol and Alcoholism.* (n.d.). Alcohol Facts and Statistics. Available at: https://www.niaaa.nih.gov/alcohol-health/overview-alcohol-consumption/alcohol-facts-and-statistics. [Accessed 12 June 2019].

[4] Fomby, Paula and Cherlin, Andrew. (April 2007). Family Instability and Child Well-Being. *National Center for Biotechnology Information.* Available at: https://www.ncbi.nlm.nih.gov/pmc/articles/PMC3171291/. [Accessed 12 June 2019].

[5] Waldfogel, Jane et al. (Fall 2010). Fragile Families and Child Wellbeing. *National Center for Biotechnology Information.* Available at: https://www.ncbi.nlm.nih.gov/pmc/articles/PMC3074431/. [Accessed 12 June 2019].

[6] Gorman, Gregory et al. (Dec. 2010). Wartime Military Deployment and Increased Pediatric Mental and Behavioral Health Complaints. *AAP News & Journals Gateway.* Available at: https://pediatrics.aappublications.org/content/126/6/1058.full?sid=68724893-acce-4f05-b329-4096865038cc. [Accessed 12 June 2019].

[7] Siegel, Benjamin et al. (June 2013). Health and Mental Health Needs of Children in US Military Families. *American Academy of Pediatrics.* Available at: https://pediatrics.aappublications.org/content/pediatrics/early/2013/05/22/peds.2013-0940.full.pdf. [Accessed 12 June 2019].

[8] Thomas, Alexander et al. (n.d.) The New York Longitudinal Study Alexander Thomas, Stella Chess, Herbert G. Birch personality types —temperament traits. *The Age of Sage.* Available at: https://www.age-of-the-sage.org/psychology/chess_thomas_birch.html. [Accessed 12 June 2019].

[9] Allard, Lindsey and Hunter, Amy. (Oct. 2010). Understanding Temperament in Infants and Toddlers. *Center on the Social and Emotional Foundations for Early Learning.* Available at: http://csefel.vanderbilt.edu/resources/wwb/wwb23.html. [Accessed 12 June 2019].

[10] Keogh, Barbara. (March 2019). How temperament affects parents, children, and family life. *GreatSchools.* Available at: https://www.greatschools.org/gk/articles/temperament-affects-parents-children-family/. [Accessed 12 June 2019].

[11] Barnett, Melissa. (Sept. 2008). Economic Disadvantage in Complex Family Systems: Expansion of Family Stress Models. *National Center for Biotechnology Information.* Available at: https://www.ncbi.nlm.nih.gov/pmc/articles/PMC4095799/. [Accessed 12 June 2019].

www.ingramcontent.com/pod-product-compliance
Lightning Source LLC
LaVergne TN
LVHW091224080426
835509LV00009B/1154